Models of Priestly Formation

Assessing the Past, Reflecting on the Present, and Imagining the Future

Edited by Declan Marmion, Michael Mullaney, and Salvador Ryan

LITURGICAL PRESS
Collegeville, Minnesota

www.litpress.org

Scripture quotations are from New Revised Standard Version Bible © 1989 National Council of the Churches of Christ in the United States of America. Used by permission. All rights reserved worldwide.

Excerpts from the English translation of *The Liturgy of the Hours* © 1973, 1974, 1975, International Commission on English in the Liturgy Corporation (ICEL); excerpts from the English translation of *The Ordination of Deacons, Priests, and Bishops* © 1975, ICEL. All rights reserved.

Excerpts from *Ratio Fundamentalis Institutionis Sacerdotalis* © Congregation for the Clergy. Used with permission.

Excerpts from *Pastores Dabo Vobis* by John Paul II © Libreria Editrice Vaticana. Used with permission.

Excerpts from documents of the Second Vatican Council are from *Vatican Council II: Constitutions, Decrees, Declarations; The Basic Sixteen Documents*, edited by Austin Flannery, OP, © 1996. Used with permission of Liturgical Press, Collegeville, Minnesota.

© 2019 by Order of Saint Benedict, Collegeville, Minnesota. All rights reserved. No part of this book may be used or reproduced in any manner whatsoever, except brief quotations in reviews, without written permission of Liturgical Press, Saint John's Abbey, PO Box 7500, Collegeville, MN 56321-7500. Printed in the United States of America.

Library of Congress Cataloging-in-Publication Data

Names: Marmion, Declan, editor. | Mullaney, Michael J., editor. | Ryan, Salvador, editor.
Title: Models of priestly formation : assessing the past, reflecting on the present, and imagining the future / edited by Declan Marmion, Michael Mullaney, and Salvador Ryan.
Description: Collegeville, Minnesota : Liturgical Press, [2019].
Identifiers: LCCN 2019001214 (print) | LCCN 2019004690 (ebook) | ISBN 9780814664377 (eBook) | ISBN 9780814664124 (pbk.)
Subjects: LCSH: Catholic Church—Clergy—Training of.
Classification: LCC BX900 (ebook) | LCC BX900 .M58 2019 (print) | DDC 230.07/32—dc23
LC record available at https://lccn.loc.gov/2019001214

"A thought-provoking and inspiring collection of future-oriented perspectives on priestly formation from a richly diverse range of global voices—teachers and practitioners as well as senior voices from religious orders and other church leaders who share a multitude of experience at the formative coalface. Together the contributors seek to answer Pope Francis' call for the church to jettison the culture of clericalism and the pedestal model of priesthood in favor of promoting, as the editors make clear, 'a model of discipleship, service and mercy.'"

—Gerard Mannion, DPhil
Amaturo Professor in Catholic Studies, Georgetown University

"This extraordinarily helpful symposium was produced by a stellar cast of authors. High professional qualifications and years of valuable experience give great credibility to their recommendations for the human, spiritual, intellectual and pastoral dimensions of priestly formation. They envisage ministerial priesthood as nothing less than a lifelong pilgrimage of Christian discipleship and human integration. I cannot recommend this book too highly."

—Gerald O'Collins, SJ, taught for 33 years at the Gregorian University, Rome, and is now a research fellow of the University of Divinity (Melbourne)

"This is the book I've been looking for since the most recent *Ratio Fundamentalis* was promulgated in 2016! The carefully compiled essays in this volume helped me to grasp the distinctive nuances of the new *Ratio* within the wider history of priestly formation and expanded my appreciation of the global perspective we must take. As a result, I have an even greater humility regarding my own vocation as a formator."

—Dr. Ann M. Garrido
Aquinas Institute of Theology

"*Models of Priestly Formation* is of utmost importance in the ongoing discussion on Church reform and pastoral ministry. This book is particularly eye-opening as it casts a light on the vast differences in priestly formation in the long history of the Church (from Trent to Vatican II to the internet savvy and social-media connected seminarians of today) and in the new geography of global Catholicism (not only the northern hemisphere, but also Africa, Asia, and Australia), at the time of the global sex abuse crisis. Highly recommended—but it should be required reading—for all those who work in programs for the formation of priests but also lay ministers."

>—Dr. Massimo Faggioli
>Professor of Historical Theology, Villanova University

"*Models of Priestly Formation* is an essential resource for anyone undertaking this ministry today. This overview of Magisterial documents, as well as the history and theology of seminary formation is balanced by practical reflections by leading experts. The authors provide vision and offer hope in a critical moment in Church history, when healthy human and spiritual development must be guaranteed."

>—Fr. David Songy, OFMCap, STD, PsyD
>President and CEO, Saint Luke Institute, Silver Spring, Maryland

"The Tridentine Church is crumbling. Its renewal requires priests who are freed from clericalism and unafraid of mature collaboration with the laity. How are we to form such priests? There are few more important questions for Catholicism today and this book engages with it courageously and insightfully."

>—Timothy Radcliffe, OP, former Master of the Dominican Order

Contents

List of Contributors   ix

Foreword   xv
   Archbishop Eamon Martin

Introduction   xxv
   Declan Marmion, SM

Chapter One
Seminary Formation since the Council of Trent:
   A Historical Overview   1
   Salvador Ryan

Chapter Two
The Gift of the Priestly Vocation in the *Ratio Fundamentalis*
   Institutionis Sacerdotalis   23
   Jorge Carlos Patrón Wong

Chapter Three
Priestly Formation after *Pastores Dabo Vobis*   41
   Katarina Schuth, OSF

Chapter Four
A Reflection on the Qualities of Candidates Entering Seminary
   and the Formation Implications   61
   Christopher Jamison, OSB

Chapter Five
Analogia Ecclesiae—Models of Priesthood:
   Some Implications for Formation   73
    Kevin O'Gorman, SMA

Chapter Six
Training for Catholic Priesthood in Ireland Today:
   Looking Back to Look Forward   89
    Brenda Dolphin, RSM

Chapter Seven
Authenticity in Education for Ministry   105
    Aoife McGrath

Chapter Eight
An International Perspective on Priestly Formation   127
    Ronald D. Witherup, PSS

Chapter Nine
Forming the Parish-Priestly Integrated Identity   147
    John Kartje

Chapter Ten
Formation of Priests: Assessing the Past, Reflecting on the Present,
   Imagining the Future   163
    Hans Zollner, SJ

Additional Chapters Included in E-Book Edition

Chapter Eleven
Priestly Formation in Africa in the Light of the *Ratio Fundamentalis*
   Institutionis Sacerdotalis   179
    Bede Ukwuije, CSSp

Chapter Twelve
A Zambian Perspective on the Propaedeutic Year in Light of
   the Revised *Ratio Fundamentalis Institutionis Sacerdotalis*   201
   Cornelius Hankomoone, PSS

Chapter Thirteen
Challenges in the Formation of Seminarians in a Flourishing
   Indian Church: Past, Present, and Future   217
   Gabriel Mathias, OFM

Chapter Fourteen
The Challenge for Priestly Formation in Australia
   after the Royal Commission into Institutional Responses
   to Child Sex Abuse   239
   David Ranson

List of Contributors

Editors

Declan Marmion, SM, is dean of the Faculty of Theology and professor of systematic theology at St. Patrick's College, Maynooth. He is editor of the *Irish Theological Quarterly*. Recent publications include: *Remembering the Reformation: Martin Luther and Catholic Theology* [ed.] with Salvador Ryan and Gesa E. Thiessen (Minneapolis: Fortress Press, 2017).

Michael Mullaney is president of the Pontifical University and professor of canon law at St. Patrick's College, Maynooth. He received his doctorate in canon law, with specialization in rotal jurisprudence at the Gregorian University, Rome, and has served as judge of the National Marriage Appeals Tribunal of Ireland. He has lectured in canon law at a number of theological institutions, including St. Patrick's College, Thurles; Milltown Institute of Theology and Philosophy; and St. Patrick's College, Maynooth, before being appointed president in 2017. In July 2018, he hosted the 26th General Assembly of the International Federation of Catholic Universities (IFCU) at Maynooth on the theme "Catholic Universities: Working in Solidarity as Responsible Agents from the Local to the Global." He is a member of the Canon Law Society of Britain and Ireland.

Salvador Ryan is professor of Ecclesiastical History at St. Patrick's College, Maynooth. He is reviews editor of *Irish Theological Quarterly* and has published widely on late medieval and early modern popular religion and ritual. Recent publications include (with Henning Laugerud and Laura Katrine Skinnebach) *The Materiality of Devotion in Late Medieval Northern Europe: Images, Objects and Practices* (Dublin: Four Courts Press, 2016); *Death and the Irish: A Miscellany* (Dublin: Wordwell Books, 2016); and (with Liam M. Tracey) *The Cultural Reception of the Bible: Explorations in Theology, Literature and the Arts* (Dublin: Four Courts Press, 2018).

Contributors

Brenda Dolphin, RSM, has been involved in religious formation, both initial and ongoing, with priests, religious, and laypeople for the past forty years. She is widely known as a lecturer, retreat giver and facilitator and has worked in Africa, Australia and Europe. She was a professor in the Institute of Psychology at the Pontifical Gregorian University until September 2016 and is currently the postulator for the cause of the founder of her congregation.

Cornelius Hankomoone, PSS, (E-book only) is a former Zambian regional superior of the Society of the Priests of St. Sulpice, USA province. For fifteen years, he served as a member of the formation team at the propaedeutic seminary, Emmaus Spirituality Center in Lusaka, Zambia. He was the first Zambian indigenous priest to serve there as rector. He holds a doctorate in systematic theology from the Gregorian University in Rome.

Christopher Jamison, OSB, was formerly director of the National Office for Vocation, Catholic Church of England and Wales. A former abbot of Worth Abbey and headmaster of its school, he was elected abbot president of the English Benedictine Congregation in 2017.

John Kartje is rector and president of Mundelein Seminary. Ordained a priest for the Archdiocese of Chicago in 2002, he has a PhD in astrophysics from the University of Chicago, an MDiv and STB from the University of St. Mary of the Lake, and an STL and STD from the Catholic University of America. He is author of *Wisdom Epistemology in the Psalter: A Study of Psalms 1, 73, 90 and 107* (De Gruyter, 2014). Since 2009 he has served as acting president of the Pontifical Faculty of Theology, assistant professor in the Department of Biblical Studies, seminarian spiritual director, and team member of the formation faculty at Mundelein Seminary before being appointed its president in 2015.

Archbishop Eamon Martin is archbishop of Armagh and primate of all Ireland. He is chancellor of the Pontifical University, St. Patrick's College, Maynooth.

Gabriel Mathias, OFM, (E-book only) has been involved in initial and ongoing formation of priests and religious for the past 37 years. He has been a regular visiting lecturer at various seminaries and institutes of formation in India, such as St. Pius X Seminary, Mumbai; National Vocation Center, Pune; and St. Peter's Seminary and Dharmaram Pontifical Athenaeum, Bangalore. He has been the rector and teacher at his order's seminary in Bangalore as well as the vice provincial of his province and general councillor of his order in Rome.

Aoife McGrath is a lecturer in pastoral theology and parish placement coordinator at the Pontifical University, St. Patrick's College, Maynooth. She previously worked as a parish pastoral worker in the Diocese of Waterford & Lismore, and as a researcher for Catholic Bishops' Conferences in Ireland and Australia. She is a frequent speaker at parish, pastoral area, and diocesan events, addressing contemporary issues of faith, discipleship, and ministry.

Kevin O'Gorman, SMA, taught philosophy and theology throughout the 1990s in St. Peter's and St. John Vianney seminaries in Pretoria, South Africa. He has been lecturer in moral theology at

St. Patrick's College, Maynooth, since 2009. Among his relevant recent publications is "The Priest as Man of Mercy," *Doctrine & Life* (2016).

David Ranson (E-book only) is a priest of the Diocese of Broken Bay, parish priest of Holy Name, Wahroonga, and vicar general of the diocese. He was ordained in 1992 in the Cistercian monastery of Tarrawarra Abbey. For many years he has lectured through the Sydney College of Divinity at the Catholic Institute of Sydney. He is well known for his writing and lecturing throughout Australia and New Zealand on issues of spiritual and pastoral formation, and on the implications of sexual abuse within the church.

Sister Katarina Schuth, OSF, has held the Endowed Chair for the Social Scientific Study of Religion at The St. Paul Seminary School of Divinity, University of St. Thomas in Minnesota, since 1991. With the John Jay College of Criminal Justice Research Team, she cowrote the report on the clergy sexual abuse crisis in the United States for the USCCB: *The Causes and Context of Sexual Abuse of Minors by Catholic Priests in the United States, 1950-2010* (March 2011). Along with many articles and book chapters, she has written five books on seminary education and ministry, most recently *Seminary Formation: Recent History—Current Circumstances—New Directions* (Liturgical Press, 2016).

Bede Ukwuije, CSSp, (E-book only) is assistant to the superior general of the Spiritans in Rome. He belongs to the Province of Nigeria South-East. He holds a doctorate in theology (ThD) from the Institut Catholique de Paris and a PhD in theology and religious studies from the Catholic University of Leuven, Belgium. Ordained priest on 31 July 1994, he was a missionary in France for twelve years, serving as students' chaplain at the University of Rennes, chaplain of the African Migrants' Community in the Dioceses of Rennes and Nanterre, and formator at the Spiritan formation community in Clamart. He returned to Nigeria and worked as director of formation at the

Spiritan International School of Theology, Attakwu-Enugu (SIST), while teaching systematic theology both at SIST and the Institut Catholique de Paris. He is a member of the Theological Commission of the Union of Superiors General, Rome. His books include *Trinité et Inculturation* (Desclée, 2008); *The Memory of Self-Donation. Meeting the Challenges of Mission* (Paulines Africa, 2009); *God, Bible and African Traditional Religion* (SNAAP Press, 2009); *The Trinitarian God: Contemporary Challenges and Relevance* (Paulines, 2013).

Ronald D. Witherup, PSS, has been superior general of the Society of the Priests of St. Sulpice (Sulpicians) since 2008. A former formator and professor of Sacred Scripture, he has authored many books and articles on Scripture and theology, including *Gold Tested in Fire: A New Pentecost for the Catholic Priesthood* (Liturgical Press, 2012), and *Mercy and the Bible: Why It Matters!* (Paulist Press, 2018).

Jorge Carlos Patrón Wong is archbishop-bishop emeritus of Papantla and secretary for seminaries, Congregation for the Clergy, Rome.

Hans Zollner, SJ, born in Regensburg, Germany, in 1966, is a member of the Society of Jesus, currently serving as academic vice rector of the Pontifical Gregorian University in Rome. Fr. Zollner, a licensed psychologist and psychotherapist, is professor in the Gregorian University's Institute of Psychology. He is also an honorary professor in the Department of Theology and Religion at the University of Durham (England) and serves as president of the Centre for Child Protection of the Gregorian. He is a member of the Pontifical Commission for the Protection of Minors.

Foreword

Archbishop Eamon Martin
Archbishop of Armagh and Primate of All Ireland

One of Ireland's earliest mentions of priestly formation can be found in the tenth-century Rule of the *Céli Dé*. The document tells us that when the candidate has been taught how to pray the Liturgy of the Hours and "the correct method of administering Baptism and Communion," the formator is entitled to a cow from the candidate's family! In subsequent years, the formator is to be paid a calf, a pig, and four sacks of grain "together with a reasonable supply of clothing and food." When the candidate passes his final exams, his formator is entitled to "a supper, of food and beer" before the bishop, "for a party of five that night."[1]

Friends, I am confident that this International Symposium on Models of Priestly Formation will have more than enough to be getting on with if it concentrates on developments over the past fifty years! Since the Second Vatican Council's 1965 Decree on Priestly Training, *Optatam Totius*, we've had the 1970 *Ratio Fundamentalis Institutionis Sacerdotalis*; updates on this text in 1985, particularly in light of the 1983 *Code of Canon Law*; reflections on priestly formation at the

---

1. *The Rule of the Céli Dé*, ed. E. J. Gwynn, *Hermathena* 44, suppl. vol. 2. (Dublin: Hodges & Figgis, 1927).

1990 Synod of Bishops, followed by Pope St. John Paul II's important post-synodal apostolic exhortation *Pastores Dabo Vobis* (25 March 1992)—and not a mention of a cow or a calf in any of them!

Now, more than thirty years later, we have a new edition of the *Ratio*, promulgated on 8 December 2016, titled "The Gift of Priestly Vocation." The new *Ratio* envisions a paradigm shift in priestly formation which calls for a considerable rethink of the structures and relationships in priestly formation. While the conciliar and post-conciliar documents on priestly formation have provided an excellent framework for bishops and seminaries, the recent *Ratio Fundamentalis Institutionis Sacerdotalis*, together with Pope Francis's various discourses about priestly lifestyle, offers a new vision, requiring new structures—new wine requiring fresh wineskins.

At this international symposium, we are all being invited to step out of our comfort zones in order to reimagine past and existing models of formation in light of the new *Ratio*: What is the "new wine"? What are the "new wineskins"?

I hope that one of the fruits of this symposium will be to inform the preparation of a new *Ratio Nationalis* for Ireland. Episcopal Conferences are currently being tasked with redesigning and updating their programmes of priestly formation. This means not only implementing the new *Ratio* in a way that takes account of local traditions, customs and needs but also courageously moving the whole formation experience beyond past and present methods so that priests will be suitably prepared to engage with, and evangelise, the secularised contemporary culture.

The preparation and implementation of the *Ratio Nationalis* for Ireland will require the thoughtful and collegial cooperation of the bishops, in dialogue with the lay faithful (male and female) and with those experienced in formation. We will need a unified and coherent approach with regard to the various elements of formation: the prior accompaniment and discernment with candidates; the admissions process; the introduction of the propaedeutic year;

the formation structures and programme for candidates preparing for the priesthood.

Recently when a parishioner asked me, "Archbishop, where did you train to be a priest?," he quite innocently reminded me that past models of formation often emphasised the "training" of seminarians through discipline and instruction in the necessary behaviours, habits, and attitudes. The pedagogical method used in "training priests" tended to isolate candidates from the world in order to equip them with sufficient spiritual, intellectual and moral strength before they were sent back into the world to engage in the church's mission. The seminary structure and programme was inclined to emphasise order, structure and discipline. The task of seminary educators was to ensure that candidates were thoroughly grounded in theological truths and priestly spirituality with clear expectations in terms of doctrinal orthodoxy, liturgical celebration, pastoral ministry and priestly spirituality.

Equipped with this "training," we emerged after ordination into a very complex and conflicted world, where we found an increasing disconnect between what our church stood for and the prevailing culture around us.

I have often wondered, however, could any kind of priestly "training" (and I use that word "training" deliberately) have fully prepared me for what lay ahead: the seismic shift that would occur in the early 1990s in Ireland's relationship with church and with priests; the horrendous and shocking child sex abuse scandals; the challenges swept in by a wave of secularisation; the digital revolution, and arrival of the internet and social media; the tendency in society towards rampant consumerism, individualism and relativism; the struggle to live a celibate life in a hyper-sexualised culture; the challenge of maintaining good physical and mental health and well-being in an increasingly rushed, stressful and pressurised environment; the decline in vocations to the priesthood and religious life bringing increased demands and a certain loss of morale for those in ministry; enhanced expectations regarding governance and accountability for the temporal goods of the church?

Like the disciples on the road to Emmaus, many of us newly ordained priests in late 1980s Ireland talked together about all that was happening—sometimes our faces downcast; "our hope had been . . ." In the years following the council, a lot had been written about a "crisis of identity" among priests. In our early years of priesthood, with so much change in the once-familiar role and surroundings for priests, one might more accurately have spoken of a "crisis of compass" or "loss of bearings."

"Future-Proofing" Formation

Any consideration of priestly formation must see formation as a lifelong process. Who knows what challenges lie ahead for today's seminarians? How might we best prepare them for the changes that will transform the world in twenty or thirty years' time but which we cannot even dream of today? To put it in business terms: How can we "future-proof" formation?

Thankfully, the new *Ratio* can help us in this regard. It emphasises a model of priesthood as continuing discipleship, meaning that, even after ordination, formation cannot be "interrupted." "The priest not only 'learns to know Christ' but, under the action of the Holy Spirit, he finds himself within a process of gradual and continuous configuration to [Christ], in his being and his acting, which constantly challenges [him] to inner growth" (*Ratio* 80; hereafter, RF).

In this sense, the priest can never consider himself to be definitively formed. A priest is certainly not the man who arrives at a parish, perfectly packaged, with all the answers. There will often be people who are more qualified than he in facing particular problems, and the new challenges that emerge may well be beyond his seminary formation. This is why his relationship with Christ is paramount. Pope Benedict XVI once said that "the faithful expect only one thing from priests: that they be specialists in promoting the encounter between man and God."[2]

Formation in Discipleship

It has to be fundamental then, to every model of seminary, that we are all—seminarians, rectors and formators, theologians—on the lifelong journey of discipleship, called to follow Jesus Christ. Consequently, the distinctions between the steps (propaedeutic, initial, permanent), between the roles (of bishop, rector, formator, spiritual director), between the dimensions (human, spiritual, pastoral and academic) and between the stages (discipleship, configuration, pastoral) are all somewhat secondary and instrumental to the overall integral formation of each of us as pilgrims along the Sequela Christi—under the action of the Holy Spirit and sustained by the grace of God.

This reflects what Pope Francis stated in an address to the Congregation for the Clergy in October 2014: "Formation is . . . not a unilateral act by which someone transmits theological or spiritual notions. Jesus did not say to those he called: 'Come, let me explain,' 'Follow me, I will teach you': no! The formation offered by Christ to his disciples came rather as a 'come, and follow me,' 'do as I do,' and this is the method that today too, the Church wants to adopt for her ministers." Pope Francis continues: "The formation of which we speak is a discipular experience which draws one to Christ and conforms one ever more to Him. Precisely for this reason, it cannot be a limited task, because priests never stop being disciples of Jesus, who follow Him. . . . Initial and on-going formation are distinct because each requires different methods and timing, but they are two

---

[2]. Benedict XVI, Address during a meeting with the clergy at Warsaw Cathedral, 25 May 2006, http://w2.vatican.va/content/benedict-xvi/en/speeches/2006/may/documents/hf_ben-xvi_spe_20060525_poland-clergy.html.

halves of one reality, the life of a disciple cleric, in love with his Lord and steadfastly following him."[3]

Formation in discipleship helps to prepare pastors who can meet the challenges presented by Pope Francis for the priests of today: to be priests to "accompany" God's scattered people and heal their wounds, "as in a field hospital"; priests who will be shepherds who know "the smell of the sheep" and are able to serve with the mind and heart of the Good Shepherd; priests who are missionaries, witnessing to "the joy of the Gospel." (Incidentally, while the expression "missionary disciples" only appears twice in the *Ratio*, the word "missionary" seems to appear everywhere in it: "missionary spirit," "missionary zeal," "missionary impulse," "missionary joy," "missionary fervour"; the *Ratio* states that formation must be clearly "missionary in spirit," and formation structures, programmes and processes should cultivate this spirit in seminarians.)

Formation is therefore not about mastering techniques or functional roles, but about following the path of discipleship: internalising, in cooperation with divine grace, the core virtues and ideals of discipleship. Put simply, one cannot be a credible witness, shepherd, healer or proclaimer of the Good News to contemporary culture unless one is rooted in a profound relationship with Jesus with the zeal and attitudes of a disciple that will last a lifetime.

Humility and Vocational Discernment

A word of caution, however: even though one could speak of moving from "training of seminarians" to "formation in discipleship," this does not mean that formation for the priesthood loses its specificity. The church has clearly stated expectations of her priests in terms

---

3. Francis, Address to the plenary of the Congregation for the Clergy, 3 October 2014, https://w2.vatican.va/content/francesco/en/speeches/2014/october/documents/papa-francesco_20141003_plenaria-congregazione-clero.html.

of the discipline of the clergy and the understanding of the priesthood. It is my contention that nothing in the new *Ratio* is inimical to the established teaching on the ordained ministry. However, the new *Ratio* does appear to emphasise that the seminarian, and priest, through pastoral accompaniment, engagement and discernment, must seek to interiorise these doctrinal understandings so that they do not exist merely as a "veneer" over his personality.

As the *Ratio* puts it: Priestly formation involves "working humbly and ceaselessly on oneself . . . so that the priest opens himself honestly to the truths of life and to the real demands of ministry. . . . This work cannot be undertaken satisfactorily by relying only on his own human resources. On the contrary, it relies principally on welcoming the gift of divine grace" (RF 43).

A good formation programme has therefore to foster in the seminarian, and in the priest, the virtue of humility and a willingness to search both for the right answers and be open to receiving the help he needs to be a faithful disciple of Christ in a changing world. This is why the spirit of humble discernment is so important. Discernment will sometimes be painful as it requires honesty, integrity, perception, sincerity and an openness to engage with every element and all areas of formation.

Vocational discernment also requires a relationship of trust with formators, an honest assessment of one's own strengths and weaknesses and an honest and appropriate disclosure of these to formators; a willingness to receive and accept direction, guidance, correction; above all the capacity to live discipleship and priesthood consistently and systematically. This is a lifelong work project.

No "Lone Rangers"

One of the "tools for the journey" which formation must nurture is the ability to work with others. The candidate must be able to work in communion with his bishop, other priests and the members of the people of God. The candidate must always remember that he has come from the Christian community and upon ordination returns to this community (RF, Intro. 3). The days when we could consider the priest as a "lone ranger" or a "rugged individual" are long past.

St. John Chrysostom was clear in his *Six Books on the Priesthood* that "the most basic task of a Church leader is to discern the spiritual gifts of all those under his authority, and to encourage those gifts to be used to the full benefit of all. Only a person who can discern the gifts of others and can humbly rejoice at the flourishing of these gifts is fit to lead the Church."[4]

New Wineskins?

To summarise then, the "new wine" or renewed vision of seminary formation aimed at by the *Ratio* is one of ongoing "transformation," or "conversion" where seminary promotes an "internalisation" of the values and ideals of discipleship. But what of the "new wineskins"? This, friends and delegates to our symposium, is your task—to tease out the characteristics and practical models of formation needed to respond to the new *Ratio*.

Clearly the essential issue is not one of simply reforming the physical structure or location of the seminary—indeed such a preoccupation can actually divert from the real challenge of the *Ratio*. Whatever the physical shape or building, what is most important is to provide the structures and processes of formation that will foster true conversion and commitment on the part of candidates for the priesthood, as distinct from mere compliance and conformity. The new *Ratio* acknowledges four generally accepted models:

---

4. John Chrysostom, *Six Books on the Priesthood*, trans. G. W. Butterworth (Crestwood, NY: St. Vladimir's Seminary Press, 1964), 44.

1. residential seminaries where all aspects of formation are addressed

2. houses of formation with a nearby pontifical or Catholic university providing the academic courses

3. parish-based models of formation, where seminarians live in a parish supervised by a local parish priest /mentor and take their academic formation in a nearby university or pontifical university

4. "part-time" models where seminarians in the first cycle are engaged in full-time studies at various universities but come together regularly with a rector and other formators for spiritual exercises and group sessions to continue discerning their vocation before entering theology

Other models which might offer useful perspectives include the Paris Model, centred around the bishop and his cathedral, and the Redemptoris Mater model for candidates coming through the Neocatechumenal Way.

It is clear that, whatever the model or models chosen, our aim should be to ensure:

1. a quality propaedeutic experience, rooted in the cultural, ecclesial and social reality of Ireland, preceded by a period of accompaniment and discernment with an experienced priest who would be a mentor and spiritual director

2. that those admitted to a seminary formation programme should have a capacity for community life and be open to lifelong prayerful formation as disciples of Christ; all the time developing interior maturity and a clear coherence of life with their convictions

3. that the formation community is distinctive and small enough to sustain a strong sense of community while not being turned in on itself—this means having frequent and meaningful pastoral placements throughout the years of formation experience

4. that the formation team not only accompanies seminarians but is itself open to being formed in the process

5. that there is a strong relationship between formator, seminarian and bishop, with frequent conversations and contact between all three

6. that there is a greater involvement of, and collaboration with, laity—women and men—in the formation programme

7. that there is a strong emphasis on prayer, communication skills, catechetical skills, leadership and facilitation skills

8. that the seminary formation team has a broader role as a key motivator in vocations promotion and in ongoing formation throughout Ireland

Friends, I commend these thoughts to you as you begin this symposium, grateful that you have taken the time and made the effort to be part of this conversation in which we assess the past, reflect on the present and imagine the future. I cannot promise a calf, a pig, or four sacks of grain, but I trust that you will leave this symposium emboldened and informed to continue your vitally important task of helping to form men to serve Christ and his church. May God grant success to the work of our hands.

Introduction

Declan Marmion, SM

This volume on models of priestly formation arose out of an international conference on the theme at St. Patrick's College, Maynooth, Ireland, in November 2017. The new *Ratio Fundamentalis Institutionis Sacerdotalis* (The Gift of the Priestly Vocation), promulgated the previous year, served as a key document of reference. In Ireland there has been much recent discussion about the suitability of large institutional seminaries in the context of the reduced numbers of entrants. Against this backdrop, the Faculty of Theology of St. Patrick's College proposed an international conference on priestly formation which had four aims:

- to reflect on the issue of priestly formation since Vatican II
- to assess the current situation
- to look at best practice from elsewhere
- to imagine new models of priestly formation into the future

While the conference focussed primarily on the English-speaking world and on the Northern hemisphere, the editors commissioned some additional chapters (which appear in the e-version of the book) that focus on the challenges of formation in India, Africa and Australia.

In his welcoming address to the conference, Archbishop Eamon Martin, primate of all Ireland, spoke about a paradigm shift in priestly formation now taking place and how new structures of formation or "new wineskins" need to be found. This work, he said, would form part of the new *Ratio Nationalis* for Ireland and take place in a culture that has experienced some seismic shifts—the clerical sexual abuse scandals, the digital revolution, secularisation, individualisation, etc., all of which have impacted priestly vocations. Referring to the new *Ratio*, he spoke of formation as a lifelong process and the challenge to form a "disciple cleric" who is missionary in spirit.

In the opening survey chapter on priestly formation since Trent, Salvador Ryan emphasises the unevenness of seminary formation in the centuries after the council. Both the number of seminaries established, and the quality of the formation offered, varied quite considerably from region to region, depending on local circumstance. Although the decree *Cum Adulescentium Aetas* of 1563 mandated the establishment of seminaries in every diocese, it did not compel all future clergy to attend them. This meant that, for centuries afterwards, one could still proceed to ordination without having undergone a seminary education, a situation that would only change with the issuing of the Code of Canon Law in 1917. Ryan also argues that the principal focus of seminary training in the centuries after Trent was not primarily a solid formation in speculative theology (that was the business of universities) but, rather, a decent spiritual, pastoral and practical formation in the administration of the sacraments. In the final analysis, Trent's decree on seminary education was far from prescriptive, leaving many of the decisions regarding its application in individual dioceses to bishops themselves. In this regard, it was malleable and adaptable to the changing needs of a diocese over time. To speak, then, of an overarching experience of the Tridentine seminary in, certainly, the first three hundred years after its promulgation is to misunderstand its variegated nature.

In chapter 2, Jorge Carlos Patrón Wong, archbishop secretary for seminaries at the Congregation for the Clergy, describes how the new *Ratio* emerged from a long period of consultation from the "real life experiences" of seminary formation worldwide. Pope Francis's vision is that formation to the priesthood is *an experience of ongoing discipleship*, since "priests never stop being disciples of Jesus, who follow Him."[1] The renewal of the church depends in many ways on the renewal of the priesthood. Archbishop Wong discusses the stages and agents of formation in the *Ratio*, emphasizing the need for support and accompaniment not only for those recently ordained but also for middle-aged priests, who carry most of the responsibilities in dioceses and religious congregations. Finally, he reminds bishops to respect the final discernment of formation teams about a candidate—a point underlined by many of the contributors.

In chapter 3, "Priestly Formation after *Pastores Dabo Vobis*," Katarina Schuth, OSF, traces the significance and the legacy of *Pastores Dabo Vobis* in relation to its Vatican II predecessor *Optatam Totius*.[2] She notes some of the significant changes in seminary formation in recent years: the development of human formation programs, the expansion of pastoral experiences, and a sharper focus on priestly life and ministry. Three areas for further development in seminary formation conclude the chapter: an evaluation of current admission standards and procedures; how to help seminarians acquire a balanced view of the church and her members as they exist in reality; and how to develop a more thorough understanding of the impact on seminarians of secular society and culture.

Christopher Jamison, OSB, former director for the National Office of Vocation in England and Wales and now abbot president of the English Benedictines, discusses some characteristics of the "youth

---

1. Francis, Address to the Plenary of the Congregation for the Clergy, 3 October 2014.

2. Second Vatican Council, Decree on the Training of Priests (*Optatam Totius*), 28 October 1965. All quotations of Vatican II documents are taken from Austin Flannery, ed., *Vatican Council II: Constitutions, Decrees, Declarations; The Basic Sixteen Documents* (Collegeville, MN: Liturgical Press, 2014).

generation" from which seminarians come. Young people today "stay young longer," marry later, and enter seminaries later. This generation creates their own world for themselves, are "hyperconnected," and derive fellowship from social media. They have little sense of belonging to institutions, yet the seminarians from this group tend to love the Catholic Church and are seeking a clear identity. Most are "reverts" or converts and their zeal needs time to mature. Eucharist and eucharistic devotions are central. On the downside, there is a tendency towards an individualistic spirituality, seeing faith as primarily a gift for themselves rather than one to be shared with others. This can lead to narcissism and a sense of self-importance which can only be overcome via a journey of discernment, of stripping away the sense of self-sufficiency in order to help them discover the real meaning of church as community.

In chapter 5, Kevin O'Gorman, SMA, shows how a theology of priesthood can only be understood in the light of a theology of church. The relationship between church and priesthood is analogical, and he develops this argument through the application of Avery Dulles's models of the church to the priesthood. Dulles outlined five foci for describing the mystery of the church—*institution, mystical communion and herald, servant and sacrament*—and later added a sixth, the church as *community of disciples*. O'Gorman presents another—a seventh model of priesthood—inspired by the writings and witness of Pope Francis—the priest as *man of mercy*. An underlying theme both in this chapter and throughout the book is that human formation is a progressive achievement, a lifelong journey of integration and discipleship.

The themes of vocational accompaniment, spiritual direction and the role of women in seminary training are taken up in chapter 6 by Brenda Dolphin, RSM. The focus in *Pastores Dabo Vobis* and in the *Ratio* on human formation has allowed seminary formation to be personalized—tailored to the growth and development of each individual person moving at his own pace. The emphasis on human development has also led to an increased number of women being involved in seminary training. Seminarians now have the opportunity to interact with women as adult to adult and relate with them on an equal basis in an open, friendly and mature way from the outset of their formation. Dolphin also highlights the importance of the propaedeutic year where the prospective seminarian can experience a focused and extended period of common spiritual searching with others who are starting the same journey and towards the same goal. She notes the challenges faced by the transition from seminary to parish, especially when the current parish model is breaking down, and asks how such changes are finding their way into the training of the prospective priest. Finally, she questions whether the seminary setting as we know it today is the most suitable means for attaining the goals of initial formation for the diocesan priest. This question has now become acute in those countries with dwindling numbers of seminarians. In such circumstances a smaller formation locale might promote a greater sense of human and interpersonal growth and interaction.

The theme of integration in the process of seminary formation is a central focus of the new *Ratio* and in its precursor, *Pastores Dabo Vobis*. In chapter 7, Aoife McGrath takes up this issue, linking it with the notion of "authenticity." Her premise, and that of the *Ratio,* is that if seminarians, both individually and as a group, do not sufficiently "demonstrate—and not only in their external behaviour—that they have internalised an authentically priestly way of life . . . [which] is a sign of a mature choice to give themselves to following Christ in a special way," then this is an obstacle to the efficacy (and continuation) of their formation (RF 131). In other words, "the lack of a well-structured and balanced personality is a serious and objective hindrance to the continuation of formation for the priesthood" (RF 63).

The Society of St. Sulpice is an international group of diocesan priests dedicated to initial and ongoing formation of priests (and formators) on five continents. Their superior general, Ronald Witherup, PSS, draws on these international perspectives in chapter 8 to describe the various models of priestly formation currently operative and identifies four. First is the classic free-standing model of the traditional seminary where all aspects of formation are conducted in-house. This seems to be the model presumed in the new *Ratio*. Its weakness is its lack of connection to the real pastoral world outside. The second is the university model where the intellectual aspect of formation is catered for outside the seminary at a pontifical university or similar. The danger here is that the intellectual aspect can become disconnected from the other aspects of formation. The third model is the Paris parish-based model, devised by Cardinal Jean-Marie Lustiger, where seminarians are continually exposed to the realities of parish life. The downside is that there is no formation community as such (or formation team in the traditional sense). A fourth model, operating in France, is a part-time model for first cycle philosophy students who gather on certain weekends during the year and in the summer for retreats. There are also variations of the above models. While the plurality is to be commended, there is the problem of the quality of formation when numbers are either too small or too large. In many countries, especially in Africa but also in China, there is a serious dearth of resources for formation (lack of books, poor libraries, lack of formators, etc.). Witherup concludes by listing some challenges facing formation into the future. These include: how to avoid compartmentalization, how to achieve the "integration" referred to in the *Ratio,* how to better manage the transition from seminary to parish, and how to deal with clericalism, careerism and misogyny.

This theme of *integration* as a primary focus of seminary formation is also taken up in chapter 9 by John Kartje, rector of Mundelein Seminary in Chicago. Kartje describes an integration that happens on multiple levels. These include: the integration of the seminary into the diocese or dioceses; the integration of the four dimensions of seminary formation as laid out in *Pastores Dabo Vobis,* and the integration of the seminary faculty. If priests and people are to view the seminary as the "heart of the diocese" (*Optatam Totius* 5), then there need to be structures in place that facilitate good communication between the two from admission processes (involving lay collaboration) to the challenges facing the newly ordained and beyond. The chapter also looks at some practical processes (classroom pedagogy, parish-based integration and theological reflection) followed at Mundelein that enable the seminarian to integrate the various aspects of his formation—human, spiritual, theological and pastoral.

Hans Zollner, SJ, from the Centre of Child Protection at the Gregorian University in Rome, looks at the new generation of seminarians in Europe and elsewhere who are older and who are likely to have some experience of the world of work prior to entering the seminary. This is a group who are internet savvy and social-media connected, and who may have previously been in an intimate relationship. Given that seminarians are no longer a homogenous group, a more flexible and personalised approach is needed. Issues around sexuality and the living of celibacy need to be talked about in an open way. Typically, the church has dealt with sexual abuse by splitting it off or shelving it, yet the issue of safeguarding should not be relegated to a one-off workshop but treated as a normal issue that is discussed in class, homilies and retreats. He notes the challenges (also mentioned in chapter 4) of helping seminarians to move beyond narcissism and self-love to a desire to give oneself totally in the service of the kingdom. Alongside self-discipline and personal asceticism, the seminarian, paradoxically, needs to develop a strong sense of self and self-esteem to be able to withstand the various storms that are part of the journey of priesthood. Finally, in the context of the stagnation of spirituality after seminary, the seminarian needs to be convinced of the need for ongoing formation rather than the myth that with ordination he is complete.

The e-book version of the volume contains a further four, specially commissioned chapters outlining the challenges facing seminary formation in Africa, India and Australia. As mentioned by Ronald Witherup, one of the biggest challenges for seminaries in Africa (in contrast to Europe) is overcrowding. To this Bede Ukwuije, CSSp, in his chapter, adds: the lack of trained formators, the lure of money, and the challenges of intercultural living in formation communities. He highlights the call to servant leadership rather than being a clerical "chief" in a context where power is frequently abused. Cornelius Hankomoone, PSS, outlines the need and value of the propaedeutic year in Zambia. Once again there is the lack of material resources (e.g., lack of water) not to mention the lack of library resources, textbooks and of suitably trained formation personnel. The propaedeutic year nevertheless has helped prospective candidates to the seminary gain some grounding in the intellectual, spiritual and human dimensions of formation.

The importance of context is again to the fore in the chapter by Gabriel Mathias, OFM, on formation in India. Not unlike Africa with its various tribes, India's context comprises different ethnic groups, a dehumanizing caste system and multiple religions. This means that seminary formation must be "inculturated" (i.e., linked to the reality of widespread poverty) and that the seminarian is capable of entering into dialogue with those of other faiths. Mathias notes a worrying trend: namely, the decline in the intellectual standards of those in formation. And finally, the issue of safeguarding policy, while being developed by government, has yet to be fully appreciated in the Indian church.

Not only in the new *Ratio* but throughout this volume, there emerges a new vision of priesthood in terms of discipleship: configured to Christ and at the service of the people of God. The *cantus firmus* of the *Ratio* is its emphasis on the *integration* of all four dimensions of formation—human, spiritual, intellectual and pastoral. These dimensions are not separate stages but linked together in the journey of discipleship. In relation to ecclesiastical studies, Pope Francis has called for a wisdom and for a reflection "capable of formulating a guiding synthesis" (*Veritatis Gaudium*, Foreword, 4). For its part, the *Ratio* offers the church a synthesis of the rich experiences of formation since Vatican II, while at the same time encouraging a degree of creativity and originality at the local level. It serves as a "base text" to enable Episcopal Conferences to draw up their national *Ratio*. At the same time, the contributors highlight the need for ongoing evaluation and reform of seminaries and of priestly formation. Against the recent backdrop of the sexual harassment and abuse of seminarians in the United States and elsewhere, this task has become all the more urgent. Seminary formation will need to jettison the old clericalist model of church—one that perpetuated a separated, exalted and elitist priesthood—and promote in its place a model based on discipleship, service and mercy. It is our hope that the ensuing chapters will contribute to this process of radical rethinking of how best to prepare our future priests to serve the people of God.

Chapter One

Seminary Formation since the Council of Trent: A Historical Overview

Salvador Ryan

Introduction and Background to the Establishment of the Seminary System

On 27 June 1562, Sigismund Baumgartner, Duke Albrecht V of Bavaria's envoy (and a layman), was admitted to the Council of Trent. The submission he made on that day highlighted a number of concerns that arose out of an extensive visitation of clergy in Bavaria, carried out four years previously. The results were not encouraging, showing that the majority of clergy were ignorant and "infected with heresy" and that a mere three or four out of a hundred were not already married or living with concubines. Baumgartner made a number of recommendations on behalf of Duke Albrecht to the council for an improvement in the state of the church in the region. One of these concerned a reform of the clergy, the imposition of a stricter discipline on the conduct of their lives and, to counter their general ignorance, the establishment of schools for their training. In the words of John W. O'Malley, Baumgartner was the first to bring the idea of the establishment of "seminaries" to the council in an authoritative way.[1]

Of course, concern for the proper education of clergy was not particularly new. For centuries, complaints about the deficit in both the intellectual and moral standards of the clergy were commonplace. The Anglo-Saxon missionary, Boniface, famously complained in one of his letters that he encountered one Bavarian priest around 746 whose Latin was so poor that he baptised "in nomine patria et filia et spiritus sancti."[2] Charlemagne, in his *Admonitio Generalis* of 789, placed great emphasis on clerical education; in the words of Giles Brown, he wished that

> the parish clergy, from whom so much is now expected, are educated in Christian doctrine, and possess not only decent copies of the key Christian texts—biblical, canonical, penitential and liturgical—but also the literacy to use them.[3]

To this end, Charlemagne called for schools for *pueri* at monasteries and cathedrals (*Admonitio Generalis*, c. 72). Over two hundred years later, the preface to Burchard of Worms's *Decretum* refers to the collection of church law as a work of reference intended to remedy the

---

1. John W. O'Malley, *Trent: What Happened at the Council* (Cambridge, MA: Belknap Press, 2013), 184–86.

2. Ian Wood, "Religion in Pre-Carolingian Thuringia and Bavaria," in *The Baiuvarii and Thuringi: An Ethnographic Perspective*, eds. Janine Fries-Knoblach and Heiko Steuer with John Hines (Woodbridge: The Boydell Press, 2014), 326. If this bungled Latin baptismal formula meant anything at all, it might be translated as "in the name of the fatherland and the daughter and the holy spirit." Interestingly, Pope Zacharias would later take Boniface to task in a letter which rebuked him for his officiousness.

3. Giles Brown, "The Carolingian Renaissance," in *Carolingian Culture: Emulation and Imitation*, ed. Rosamund McKitterick (Cambridge: Cambridge University Press, 1994), 19.

"ignorance" of the clergy; it was "concisely assembled" in order to render it as accessible as possible even to untrained priests who might need to consult it as a work of reference. For Burchard, the ignorance of the clergy had significant consequences: for instance, "for those fleeing to the remedy of penance . . . on account . . . of the ignorance of the priests, help is in no way at hand."[4] By the Fourth Lateran Council of 1215, the formation of clergy was still high on the agenda. In its eleventh decree, Lateran IV referred to the fact that the Third Lateran Council had prescribed that in each cathedral church a suitable benefice should be provided for a master whose duty would be to train the clergy, but that "this decree, however, is very little observed in many churches."[5] The Council of 1215 reaffirmed and strengthened this decree by extending the appointment of a master to other churches with sufficient resources as well. The twenty-seventh decree of Lateran IV, which called the guidance of souls a "supreme art," ordered bishops to

> carefully prepare those promoted to priesthood and to instruct them . . . in the divine services and the sacraments of the church, so that they may be able to celebrate them correctly. But if they presume henceforth to ordain the ignorant and unformed, which can indeed be easily detected, we decree that both the ordainers and those ordained are to be subject to severe punishment.[6]

However, later experience would prove that not all bishops could be considered suitably equipped to the task of providing for the education of their clergy. Indeed, Lewis de Beaumont, bishop of Durham from 1316–33, a nobleman who was described as being "handsome but with bad feet," is a case in point. While possessing a reputation for

---

4. Greta Austin, *Shaping Church Law around the Year 1000: The Decretum of Burchard of Worms* (London and New York: Routledge, 2009), 81, 77.

5. Norman P. Tanner, ed., *Decrees of the Ecumenical Councils*, vol. 1 (London: Sheed and Ward, 1990), 240.

6. Tanner, *Decrees*, 248.

having remained chaste, he was also illiterate (*laicus*). One account describes the consequences of this:

> He did not understand Latin and had trouble pronouncing it. Thus, during his episcopal consecration when he was obliged to make his profession, he was unable to read it aloud even though he had previously been coached for many days. With difficulty and whispered promptings he finally got to the word *Metropoliticae* [Metropolitan]. After stuttering over it a bit, he still could not pronounce it; so he said in French "let it stand as I've read it." Everyone around him was thunderstruck, mortified that this sort of fellow was being consecrated a bishop.[7]

On the eve of the Reformation, the Fifth Lateran Council was also concerned about continual oversight of those in priestly ministry, especially those who were licensed to preach. In its eleventh session on 19 December 1516, it decreed that nobody should be allowed to carry out this office without prior examination from a superior "and unless he is found to be fit and suitable for the task by his upright behaviour, age, doctrine, honesty, prudence and exemplary life."[8] These characteristics were precisely the qualities that would be expected of candidates for formation to the priesthood in the Tridentine seminary system. Perhaps most damningly of all, the *Consilium de emendanda Ecclesia,* commissioned by and read to Pope Paul III on 9 March 1537, "identified the ordination of unsatisfactory priests as the primary cause of the ills of the Church."[9]

---

7. Geoffrey Coldingham, Robert Graystanes, and William Chambre, eds., *Historiae Dunelmensis Scriptores Tres* (London: J. B. Nichols, 1839), 118–19. Cited in John Shinners and William H. Dohar, eds., *Pastors and the Care of Souls in Medieval England* (Notre Dame, IN: University of Notre Dame Press, 1998), 48.

8. See Tanner, *Decrees.*

9. Frans Ciappara, "Trent and the Clergy in Late Eighteenth-Century Malta," *Church History* 78:1 (March 2009), 1.

Although both local and ecumenical councils of the church had decried the ignorance of the clergy through the Middle Ages, and certain minimum requirements for ordination had been laid down—such as legitimate birth and being of good moral character and, as in the case of Lateran IV and Lateran V, for instance, knowledge of specific formulae and prayers (the Ten Commandments, Our Father and Hail Mary), it would not be until after 1563 that institutions emerged whose main purpose was the professional formation of Catholic clergy.

Establishment of Seminaries in the Early Modern Period

The Council of Trent's *Cum adolescentium aetas* (canon 18), promulgated during its twenty-third session, mandated that every diocese was to provide a college for the education particularly of poor boys to the priesthood, which would enable them to read and write sufficiently well to allow them to adequately administer the sacraments. In these diocesan seminaries, boys who were to be at least twelve years old were to study "Latin grammar, sacred Scripture, ecclesiastical books, the homilies of the saints, and the things necessary for the administration of the sacraments, especially confession" and local clergy, including their bishops, were to be their instructors, or they should choose other "competent substitutes."[10] It is important to note that, in founding seminaries, Trent was mainly thinking of supporting poor boys who could not otherwise receive an education. Seminaries might admit candidates from more well-heeled families, but these would have to pay for their accommodation.[11] The seminary

---

10. Thomas B. Deutscher, "From Cicero to Tasso: Humanism and the Education of the Novarese Parish Clergy (1565–1663)," *Renaissance Quarterly* 55 (2002): 1007; Kathleen Comerford, "Italian Tridentine Diocesan Seminaries: A Historiographical Study," *Sixteenth Century Journal* 29:4 (1998): 1000.

11. Joseph Bergin, *Church, Society and Religious Change in France, 1580–1730* (New Haven, CT: Yale University Press, 2009), 195.

that Trent created is defined by Kathleen Comerford (building on a previous definition by John W. O'Malley) as

> a freestanding and programmatically integral institution reserved exclusively for the professional pastoral training of the future diocesan clergy under the direct jurisdiction of the local bishop and the academic and disciplinary staff of regular and secular clergy he hired to administer it.[12]

Although there had been long-standing concerns for the proper education of clergy, a more immediate impetus for the establishment of seminaries can be traced to the actions of Cardinal Giovanni Morone, who encouraged the Jesuits to open the Collegium Germanicum in Rome in 1552 for the education of young men from the empire who wished to be priests.[13] Cardinal Reginald Pole of England had also recognised the solution to the competency deficit among clergy to lie in the establishment of special schools, and the wording of his canon to this effect in *De Reformatione Angliae* (the decrees of his legatine synod of 1555–56) anticipates the twenty-third session of the Council of Trent by seven years.[14] Other figures such as the Andalusian priest, Juan de Avila, had opened schools for religious

---

12. Comerford, "Italian Tridentine Diocesan Seminaries," 1009. And yet such an institution did not exist in many areas for a considerable period of time after the promulgation of the 1563 decree which is customarily understood to have established the "seminary system."

13. O'Malley, *Trent*, 212. See especially Urban Fink, "The Society of Jesus and the Early History of the Collegium Germanicum, 1552–1584," in Liam Chambers and Thomas O'Connor, eds., *Catholic Communities Abroad: Education, Migration and Catholicism in Early Modern Europe* (Manchester: Manchester University Press, 2018), 34–54.

14. Comerford, "Italian Tridentine Diocesan Seminaries," 1001; O'Malley, *Trent*, 212. There had been some pre-Reformation seminary-like institutions in existence: most notably the College of the Holy Spirit in Louvain, founded in 1445; the Almo Collegio Capranica, founded in Rome in 1457; and the Geor-

instruction as early as the 1530s and had written *Memoriales* to the Council of Trent, detailing his ideas on clerical education.[15] When Duke Albrecht V of Bavaria's envoy, Sigismund Baumgartner, entered the council chamber on 27 June 1562, with the recommendation of establishing schools for the training of clergy, he was therefore expressing what had already been recognised by many others as a pressing need within the context of church reform.

With regard to *Cum adolescentium aetas*, John W. O'Malley has stated that "it is difficult to exaggerate the canon's long-range influence."[16] But the wording is important here; canon 18's influence was *long-range* rather than immediate. Adriano Prosperi has cautioned against concluding that the establishment of the seminary system transformed "ignorant, unprepared and immoral clergy" into exemplary models of priesthood overnight.[17] There was a great deal of regional diversity not only between core and peripheries but also within core Catholic countries. Marc Forster, in his study of the Diocese of Speyer, remarks how "the peasant-priest of the mid-sixteenth century only slowly evolved into the educated professional of the eighteenth."[18] Much of this could be attributed to the practical difficulties surrounding the setting up of seminaries in the first place. These colleges cost money, and bishops of dioceses were now faced not only with finding the funds necessary to establish and then maintain a seminary but also the necessity of recruiting both staff

---

gianum in Ingolstadt, established in 1492. See Fink, "The Society of Jesus and the Early History of the Collegium Germanicum," 36.

15. See David Coleman, "Moral Formation and Social Control in the Catholic Reformation: The Case of San Juan de Avila," *Sixteenth Century Journal* 26:1 (Spring 1995): 17–30.

16. O'Malley, *Trent*, 212.

17. Ciappara, "Trent and the Clergy," 2.

18. Marc Forster, *The Counter-Reformation in the Villages: Religion and Reform in the Bishopric of Speyer, 1560–1720* (Ithaca, NY, and London: Cornell University Press, 1992), 59.

and students. Kathleen Comerford points to the uneven distribution of seminaries on the Italian peninsula: for instance, less than half of the Italian dioceses opened seminaries in the sixteenth century and some Italian dioceses failed to open a seminary all through the seventeenth century.[19] The holding of diocesan or provincial synods often provided the impetus for the establishment of seminaries.[20] But in some regions, seminaries that had already been established were extinguished as a result of the upheaval of the age. Joseph Bergin, for instance, records how "the few French seminaries founded after Trent did not survive the religious wars, and a new wave of foundations only began in the 1630s."[21] Meanwhile, the first seminary was not established in Malta until as late as 1703.[22]

It is worth remembering that the notion of a "typical" Tridentine seminary in this period is misleading. These institutions could vary considerably in their fundamental *raison d'être*, student body, teaching arrangements, length of course of study, curriculum, and living arrangements. So, for example, Douai College, established by Cardinal William Allen in 1568, was the first Tridentine seminary for English speakers; and yet it was much more than that, having been founded as an educational establishment for young English Catholic scholars, both clerical students and the sons of lay gentry, who could no longer attend Oxford and Cambridge in the reign of Elizabeth I and thereby sought a Catholic education abroad.[23] Likewise, a minority of Irish students from well-heeled families pursued their clerical for-

---

19. Comerford, "Italian Tridentine Diocesan Seminaries," 1002.
20. Comerford, 1003.
21. Thomas Worster, *Seventeenth-Century Cultural Discourse* (Berlin and New York: De Gruyter, 1997), 89.
22. Ciappara, "Trent and the Clergy," 23.
23. Eamon Duffy, "Introduction: Historical," *Treasures of Ushaw College*, ed. James E. Kelly (Durham University: Scala Arts & Heritage Publishers, 2015), 17. I am grateful to James Kelly for having reminded me of this very useful volume.

mation abroad in Irish colleges located in Spain, the Low Countries, France and Italy. While Trent may have ideally envisaged grouping candidates for priesthood around their bishop in a diocesan setting for moral and spiritual formation, this was not the reality for many Irish clerical students in the seventeenth century. Thomas O'Connor adverts to the fact that, in this instance, lack of episcopal oversight was taken for granted by the Holy See and that in 1626 a papal bull allowed for the ordination of Irish clerics on the word of a college superior on the continent, thus severing a vital link between a cleric and his bishop. Furthermore, many of the colleges attended by the Irish abroad were under Jesuit, as opposed to episcopal, governance and operated independently of the hierarchy.[24] In other instances, such as at the seminary at Pavia, Jesuit lecturers in philosophy were hired in the 1640s and 1650s while the college remained a diocesan, rather than a Jesuit, seminary.[25] In eighteenth-century Lombardy, the seminary served merely as a boarding school (*convitto*), while the teaching was delivered externally in colleges run by the religious orders, a common model for seminaries in university towns.[26]

Furthermore, what might today be termed the projected "learning outcomes" of an early modern seminary education were reasonably modest; certainly in respect of a thorough grounding in theology. The seminary's principal focus was to form young men into persons capable of attending to the *cura animarum*. This did not necessarily require a deep understanding of theology. Instead, students were to be instructed in "the things necessary to know for salvation," i.e., practical, pastoral and sacramental theology, with a focus on moral and ethical behaviour. Their function should be clearly distinguished from

---

24. See especially Thomas O'Connor, "The Domestic and International Roles of Irish Overseas Colleges, 1590–1800," in Chambers and O'Connor, eds., *Catholic Communities Abroad*, 93.

25. Comerford, "Italian Tridentine Diocesan Seminaries," 1008.

26. Ciappara, "Trent and the Clergy," 23.

that of the universities where one might study theology at a much higher level. In this respect, seminaries might better be understood as technical schools for the professional training of future or already ordained clergy.[27] Indeed, they were intended precisely to provide a better (if modest) theological and spiritual formation for those who could not attend a university than they would otherwise receive; O'Malley pointedly identifies seminary formation as "an almost fall-back alternative for those who could not do better."[28] Leo Kenis remarks that "the top priority for future priests was to train them to be pious, morally upright worship leaders and parish administrators. The requirements for pursuing this model were complimented with a modicum of intellectual formation."[29] Timothy Tackett has observed that seminarians might even be discouraged from wandering into the potentially dangerous waters of speculative theology, raising subjects that might only arouse the idle curiosity of their parishioners: what the common people needed was milk, not solid food.[30] Kathleen Comerford has uncovered important clues about the content and

---

27. Comerford, "Italian Tridentine Diocesan Seminaries," 1009.

28. Klaus Ganzer, "Das Trienter Konzil und die Errichtung von Priesterseminarien," in Klaus Ganzer, et al., *Kirche auf dem Weg durch die Zeit. Institutionelles Werden und theologisches Ringen* (Münster: Aschendorff, 1997), 485; O'Malley, *Trent*, 213. I am grateful to Charlotte Methuen for this first reference.

29. Leo Kenis, "Movements toward Renewal: The Belgian Church and the Improvement of Clerical Education 1830–1850," *Nederlands Archief voor Kerkgeschiedenis / Dutch Review of Church History* 83:1 (2003): 371.

30. Timothy Tackett, *Priest and Parish in Eighteenth-Century France: A Social and Political Study of the Curés in a Diocese of Dauphiné, 1750–1791* (Princeton, NJ: Princeton University Press, 1977), 81. Dissuasion from entering into disputations for which one might be ill-prepared was a common warning for both laity and clergy in a period when "a little knowledge" might well be regarded as an eternally dangerous thing. See Salvador Ryan, " 'New Wine in Old Bottles': Implementing Trent in Early Modern Ireland," in Thomas Herron and Michael Potterton, eds., *Ireland in the Renaissance, c.1540–1660* (Dublin: Four Courts Press, 2006), 127.

purpose of a seminary education from inventories of the library of the diocesan seminary of Fiesole, taken in 1646, 1703–1715 and 1721. On the assumption that an institution may be known through its books, Fiesole's collection suggests that the educational emphasis was pastoral rather than intellectual in nature. It is interesting to note, for instance, that between 1646 and 1721 "the number of books on the study of Scripture declined sharply and controversial theology disappeared entirely. On the other hand, books on pastoral theology increased significantly as did books on private devotion."[31] Once again, however, it would be unwise to draw general conclusions from a single institution. As in so much concerning the seminary system, there was a great deal of variation from region to region.

Hubert Wolf notes that in the Tridentine church, three possible routes for training for the priesthood existed: the diocesan seminary, another (higher) school, or the university theology faculties.[32] There might, of course, be added a fourth route; which was simply that largely pursued in the Middle Ages—the apprentice system of learning "on the job," so to speak, from one's own local priest, who himself had been similarly trained up. And because attendance at seminary was not a requirement for ordination to priesthood until as late as 1917, this kind of formation also persisted through the early modern period. Franz Ciappara puts this rather starkly when he reminds us that while "Trent decreed that each diocese must have such institutions, future clergy were not compelled to attend them, and young men could still proceed to the priesthood much as before."[33] Indeed,

---

31. Kathleen Comerford, "What Did Early Modern Priests Read? The Library of the Seminary of Fiesole, 1646–1721," *Libraries and Culture* 34:3 (Summer 1999): 203, 206.

32. Hubert Wolf, "Priesterausbildung zwischen Universität und Seminar. Zur Auslegungsgeschichte des Trienter Seminardekrets," *Römische Quartalschrift für Christliche Altertumskunde und Kirchen-geschichte* [Freiburg im Breisgau] 88 (1993), 231–32. I am grateful to Charlotte Methuen for this reference.

33. Ciappara, "Trent and the Clergy," 24.

Kathleen Comerford's work on Fiesole has shown that from 1635 to 1675, about 59 percent of the priests ordained in Fiesole spent no time at all in seminary—"They were, for the most part, locals who remained local."[34] For roughly the same period, Charlotte Methuen has observed that "in the German dioceses, the main qualification of prince-bishops continued to be their birth."[35]

Furthermore, on account of Trent's non-requirement of seminary attendance or theological training prior to ordination, it was customary for many students from Britain and Ireland, who travelled for a clerical education to the continental colleges, to be ordained in advance in order that they might be in a position to help cover college fees through the acceptance of Mass stipends. And even those who did manage to attend seminary were not guaranteed to emerge as polished Tridentine specialists. Patrick J. Corish, in commenting on the poor reputations of some Irish seminarians at the Irish College in Rome in the seventeenth century, mentions, as examples, "Terence Kelly, one of the original students, who seems to have worn the Tridentine reform very lightly, or James Stafford, who entered in 1653, self-willed and a bit of a fool, or Hugh McKean, who came in 1675, self-willed and more than a bit of a knave."[36] As early as 1644,

---

34. Kathleen M. Comerford, "Clerical Education, Catechesis, and Catholic Confessionalism: Teaching Religion in the Sixteenth and Seventeenth Centuries," in *Early Modern Catholicism: Essays in Honour of John W. O'Malley*, Kathleen M. Comerford and Hilmar M. Pabel, eds. (Toronto: University of Toronto Press, 2001), 252.

35. Charlotte Methuen, "The Theologians: Who Were They?," in Kenneth Appold and Nelson H. Minnich, eds., *The Cambridge History of Reformation Theology* (forthcoming). I am grateful to Charlotte Methuen for having provided me with an advance copy of her article.

36. Patrick J. Corish, review of *The Irish College, Rome 1628–1687: An Early Manuscript Account of the Foundation and Development of the Ludovisian College of the Irish in Rome*, Albert McDonnell, ed. (Rome: Pontifical Irish College, 2003), in *The Furrow* (January 2004): 57.

Vincent de Paul, founder of the Congregation of the Mission (Vincentians), sounded a rather pessimistic note regarding the success of the seminary system up to that point: "the decree of the Council of Trent must be respected because it is of the Holy Spirit. Yet experience shows that the manner in which it is implemented in respect of the age of the seminarians means that it does not work, neither in Italy nor in France."[37] De Paul personally favoured a model implemented by Adrien Bourdoise, *curé* of St. Nicolas-du-Chardonnet in Paris, who experimented with the idea of the coming together of a community of past and future clergy and who would use his own parish as a laboratory for formation in, and practice of, the requisite pastoral skills for the priestly life. Here, then, for de Paul, the best learning took place, arising, as it did, out of experience.[38]

Ronnie Po-chia Hsia stresses that clerical discipline was imposed unevenly and with difficulty over a long period of time.[39] Testament to this is the report of one particularly amorous Maltese priest, Don Andrea Borg from St Helen's, who stated in 1789 that "he contemplated going to Turkey to apostatize to Islam and there 'take as many wives as my strength allowed me.' "[40] By as late as the turn of the twentieth century, reports of clerical behaviour did not offer more encouraging news, particularly in some Latin American regions where the seminary system was not as firmly established. Cardinal Rafael Merry del Val, papal secretary of state, listed the deficiencies of the clergy of Argentina, Uruguay and Paraguay as follows in 1907:

---

37. Bergin, *Church, Society and Religious Change in France*, 196–97.
38. Bergin, 197.
39. R. Po-chia Hsia, *The World of Catholic Renewal, 1540–1770* (Cambridge: Cambridge University Press, 1998), 120–21.
40. Ciappara, "Trent and the Clergy," 11. This was not uncommon. See Robert C. Davis, *Christian Slaves, Muslim Masters: White Slavery in the Mediterranean, the Barbary Coast, and Italy, 1500–1800* (Basingstoke, UK: Palgrave MacMillan, 2003), 90.

the Gospel is not explained; they do not teach the catechism to the faithful; they do not administer the sacraments if there is no profit in it; they do not attend to the dying promptly . . . [and] finally, not a few live in concubinage and publicly maintain illicit relationships.[41]

Clearly, then, nearly 350 years after the decree establishing the seminary system, there was still a great deal of ironing out to be done on the issue of clerical formation for ministry.

Refining the Seminary Experience into the Modern Period

The Council of Trent had attributed the spread of Protestantism in Europe in large part to the ignorance and immorality of Catholic clergy.[42] And how the clergy behaved had a direct impact on the behaviour of the laity more generally; this was expressed in clear terms by Jean-Pierre Camus, consecrated bishop of Belley (1609–1628) by St François de Sales, who remarked that priests

> must order their life like a clock, for what a clock is to a city, so is a priest; if the clock is "out of order," business, meals, and everything go astray; if the priest is disordered the laity will follow his example.[43]

The seventeenth century would see an enormous contribution to seminary development from the so-called French school of spirituality with figures such as Pierre de Bérulle, Charles de Condren, Vincent de Paul, and Jean Jacques Olier developing a spirituality for

---

41. Lisa M. Edwards, "Latin American Seminary Reform: Modernization and the Preservation of the Catholic Church," *The Catholic Historical Review* 95:2 (April 2009): 270.

42. Deutscher, "From Cicero to Tasso," 1007.

43. Worster, *Seventeenth-Century Cultural Discourse*, 89.

diocesan priests. Vincent de Paul's Congregation of the Mission, founded in 1625, and Olier's Society of St Sulpice, formed in 1641, would place special emphasis on the spiritual formation of candidates for priesthood. In his first encyclical (*E Supremi apostolatus*, 1903), Pope Pius X would note that "as a general rule, the faithful will be such as are those whom you call to the priesthood."[44]

It would be four Sulpician priests who would open the first diocesan seminary in the United States at Baltimore in 1791. In order to financially support the seminary, which had few students at the outset, the Sulpicians were to open an affiliate lay college in 1805.[45] In 1833 the second Provincial Council of Baltimore reminded itself of the duty of establishing seminaries as laid down by Trent. They considered various models: that of a bishop training seminarians at his own residence; training taking place in the cathedral rectory; and the option of training seminarians in an institution that also provided a Catholic school for lay students. One of the problems identified by the early 1850s was that each bishop wanted his own diocesan seminary, even if problems with numbers and also staffing issues made this less than ideal. At the First Plenary Council of Baltimore in 1852, while bishops urged the formation of diocesan seminaries, they also recommended the establishment of provincial seminaries where this was not possible. This gave rise to "freestanding seminaries" which ceased to rely on lay colleges for the necessary financial support.[46] In Belgium in the 1830s, provincial seminaries were where one sent one's most promising students to complete their theological studies, and

---

44. Edwards, "Latin American Seminary Reform," 269.

45. Joseph M. White, "Perspectives on the Nineteenth-Century Diocesan Seminary in the United States," *U.S. Catholic Historian* 19:1 (Winter 2001): 22–23. In its early years, the Irish seminary at Maynooth College, founded in 1795, also ran a lay college, but this only lasted from 1800 to 1817, by which time the neighbouring Jesuit school, Clongowes Wood College, had opened.

46. White, "Perspectives on the Nineteenth-Century Diocesan Seminary," 24.

this would lead, in 1834, to the establishment of a Catholic University.[47] In another adaptation of the Tridentine model, the Benedictines became responsible for the running of seminaries training candidates for the diocesan priesthood at St Meinrad Abbey in southern Indiana in 1854 and at St John's Abbey, Collegeville, in 1857.[48]

Despite such progress, the unevenness of the working out of the Tridentine seminary system was still in evidence. Archbishop John Hughes of New York was quite candid about the quality of his priests when he remarked, in 1858, "if anyone looks for extraordinary eloquence in the pulpit, or immense erudition, or able writers among the clergy of New York, he may be prepared for much disappointment." Meanwhile, the rector of the seminary in Cincinnati admitted that often candidates were ordained after just a year of theology.[49] When the nuncio to Brazil, Archbishop Gaetano Bedini, visited the United States in 1854, he advocated the setting up of an American College in Rome, which he felt would strengthen the Roman Catholic spirit, allow the Holy See to get to know the American clergy better and, not least, put an end to the worrisome business of seminarians returning home for the summer holidays, a practice that often proved fatal to their perseverance in the seminary.[50] This point was reinforced by Cardinal Johannes Franzelin of Propaganda Fide in the 1880s when he referred to the fact that, in these instances, the young men were "indulged by all" and made "continual journeys on horseback, went hunting, and what is worse, went to beach resorts, dressed entirely as laymen."[51] This eagerness to keep seminarians removed from society

---

47. Kenis, "Movements Toward Renewal," 375.
48. White, "Perspectives on the Nineteenth-Century Diocesan Seminary," 25.
49. White, "Perspectives on the Nineteenth-Century Diocesan Seminary," 26.
50. White, "Perspectives on the Nineteenth-Century Diocesan Seminary," 28. The archbishop would get his wish in 1859 when the American College in Rome opened with twelve students from eight dioceses.
51. White, "Perspectives on the Nineteenth-Century Diocesan Seminary," 31–32.

was favoured in Germany by bishops like Karl August von Reisach (1800–1869), who praised the exclusive theological training in a seminary, "away from the world" (rather than in a university setting), and under close episcopal surveillance. His seminary at Eichstätt had become a model of ultramontane clerical education before 1848.[52] Of course, there was always the danger of seminarians who were too sheltered from the world, experiencing a rude wake-up call when transitioning to the realities of pastoral life. In some instances, this transition was not made any easier for seminarians when the form of training they received did not easily translate to parish ministry on the ground. A former professor of Theology at Maynooth in the 1850s, in the context of commenting on an often excessive rigorism found in the seminary, opined later that "as a result of his training at Maynooth and faced with the realities of life 'the priest is forced to tone down . . . the principles of too rigorous a morality.'"[53]

An educational standoff, of sorts, had also taken place in the years leading up to Belgian independence in 1831. During the period of the Kingdom of the Netherlands, King William I had wished to centralise the philosophical education of future clergy in the state-run *Collegium Philosophicum*, which was then boycotted by church leaders who greatly resented what they regarded as state interference. Belgian clerics were largely looked down on by Dutch government officials who stated that "they exhibited an *air stupide* and were unable to behave

---

52. Claus Arnold, "Internal Church Reform in Catholic Germany," in *The Churches: The Dynamics of Religious Reform in Northern Europe, 1780–1920*, Joris van Eijnatten and Paula Yates, eds. (Leuven University Press, 2010), 171. See also Erich Garhammer, *Seminaridee und Klerusbildung bei Karl August Graf von Reisach—eine pastoralgeschichtliche Studie zum Ultramontanismus des 19. Jahrhunderts*, Münchener kirchenhistorische Studien, Bd. 5; Diss. Universität Regensburg 1989 (Stuttgart/Berlin/Köln, 1990). My thanks to Astrid Schilling for this last reference.

53. Michael Turner, "The French Connection with Maynooth College, 1795–1855," *Studies: an Irish Quarterly Review* 70:277 (Spring 1981): 81–82.

properly in any society."[54] Despite the drive to keep seminarians insulated from wider society, most American seminarians would continue to be educated in their own country. In 1884, Archbishop John Ireland, upon assuming responsibility for the St. Paul Diocese, made his first priority a well-run seminary, for, as he noted in a pastoral letter ten years later, he saw it as the bishop's major responsibility to provide a "numerous, learned and holy clergy."[55] It is interesting to note, too, that in a series of reports sent to Rome in 1869, on the eve of the First Vatican Council, regarding the situation of the Belgian church, it was issues such as "the spirit in the institutions, personal piety, the discipline at the seminaries" that loomed large rather than complaints about the quality of intellectual formation.[56]

In roughly the same time period, other regions were playing catch-up. Across Latin America in the second half of the nineteenth century there were many dioceses without seminaries, while those that did exist were often not fit for the purpose.[57] For one thing, there needed to be a much longer period of preparation for priesthood. In 1883, Monsignor Ignacio Montes de Oca, bishop of Monterrey, Mexico, recommended eleven years' preparation in order to be sufficiently equipped to preach effectively and to have enough English to minister to foreigners and to convert Protestants. Failing this, he warned, you will see a priest "in the pulpit if, in fact, we see him, contorting and gesturing ridiculously, speaking in such a low voice that no one

54. Kenis, "Movements toward Renewal," 373n4.
55. Daniel P. O'Neill, "The Development of an American Priesthood: Archbishop John Ireland and the Saint Paul Diocesan Clergy, 1884–1918," *Journal of American Ethnic History* 4:2 (Spring 1985): 39.
56. Kenis, "Movements toward Renewal," 387.
57. Edwards, "Latin American Seminary Reform," 267. Contrast this with the fact that in thirty-one dioceses established across the United States in 1851, most bishops had established their own seminaries. White, "Perspectives on the Nineteenth-Century Diocesan Seminary," 23.

hears him, or in excessive shouting that horrifies the audience."[58] The Latin American College, which opened in Rome in 1858, one year before its North American counterpart, would become, over time, a model for seminary reform at home.[59] And yet, while clear progress was made, problems persisted on the ground. In some regions, the shortage of clerical vocations was directly attributed by church leaders to the poor quality of existing clergy which scandalised the faithful and did little to encourage men to consider priesthood as an option. And even those who did enter seminary were wholly unprepared for a priestly life. A report written in 1911 by the rector of the Conciliar Seminary of La Paz (Bolivia) stated that "many of the boys who come to us from the provinces have witnessed acts [that were] sometimes scandalous by their parish priests and enter the Seminary [ill-prepared], ignorant even of doctrine. Very far from being inclined to the priesthood, they have [other] aspirations."[60] Meanwhile, Pope Pius X instructed the archbishop of Caracas, Venezuela, to ensure that the Venezuelan seminaries taught future priests "the virtues necessary to the priesthood, including piety, chastity, and Christian humility; good discipline and the necessary knowledge to perform their functions."[61]

Returning to the situation in North America, in 1884 the Third Plenary Council of Baltimore shifted the emphasis from a local determination of the seminary's needs and directed it to adhere to a national set of standards.[62] It also began to emphasise neglected subjects such as biblical studies, church history and homiletics. While a chair in ecclesiastical history had been established at the Irish seminary of Maynooth (at one stage in the mid-nineteenth century, the largest

58. Edwards, 271.
59. Edwards, 272.
60. Edwards, 265.
61. Edwards, 269.
62. White, "Perspectives on the Nineteenth-Century Diocesan Seminary," 34.

seminary in the world) as early as 1845, nevertheless, "the subject only played a limited part in what was a very crowded curriculum."[63] With Pope Benedict XV's issuing of a Code of Canon Law in 1917, greater uniformity was imposed on seminary formation:

> The Code prescribed the years of study at six each for minor and major seminary courses, named seminary officials, and listed the subjects to be covered in the curriculum; it laid down principles for the spiritual formation of seminarians and, crucially, it, at last, made seminary training a condition for ordination.[64]

In Joseph White's words, "Trent's principle of the bishop as responsible for directing his seminary was transformed to make him the local agent of Roman authority."[65]

Conclusion

In retrospect, what is perhaps most remarkable about the Tridentine decree of 1563, which established what could only much later be regarded as the "seminary system," is simply how it shies away from setting out in any detail how these new institutions should operate in practice. Questions, such as how long a seminary programme should last; what subjects should be taught; whether all clerical students from a diocese should attend the seminary; or, most crucially of all, whether a seminary education should be mandatory for all who wished to proceed to ordination, remained unanswered or

---

63. White, 33; Jacqueline Hill, "Laying the Nineteenth-Century Foundations: Contributions from a Catholic and a Protestant Scholar in the 1820s," in Jacqueline Hill and Mary Ann Lyons, eds., *Representing Irish Religious Histories: Historiography, Ideology and Practice* (London: Palgrave Macmillan, 2017), 59.

64. White, "Perspectives on the Nineteenth-Century Diocesan Seminary," 35.

65. White, 35.

perhaps, more precisely, were delegated to the authority of the local bishop. In essence, "the primacy of the local church's needs stands out as a central characteristic of the diocesan seminary."[66] It is this approach which rendered the Tridentine seminary such a malleable institution over the succeeding centuries, capable of adapting itself to local needs as was deemed fit. It is also, of course, what perpetuated the variegated and uneven nature of priestly formation globally right up to the twentieth century. As we imagine the future—and ask ourselves what might be the most effective models of formation for seminarians in a rapidly changing society—we could do worse than look to Trent's original decree of 1563, not as the bringing to birth of a monolithic Tridentine seminary structure but rather as a remarkably flexible piece of legislation that allowed for a variety of training models which were adapted to service the needs of the local church. With the right degree of care, and attentiveness to the lessons of the past, this should give us much to be hopeful about for the years ahead.[67]

66. White, 22.
67. I am very grateful to Thomas O'Connor for agreeing to read a draft of this chapter and for his valuable suggestions.

Chapter Two

The Gift of the Priestly Vocation in the *Ratio Fundamentalis Institutionis Sacerdotalis*

Jorge Carlos Patrón Wong
Archbishop Secretary for Seminaries Congregation for the Clergy

Introduction

It was St. Colmcille who initiated the movement known as the *peregrinatio pro Christo*, and as his biographer Adamnán informs us, he went to the Island of Iona, wishing to be *a pilgrim for Christ*. The Second Vatican Council used the term *pilgrimage* to speak about the church on earth (LG 48) and in heaven (GS 57).[1] The new *Ratio Fundamentalis Institutionis Sacerdotalis* makes use of a synonymous term to speak about the Christian life and more specifically, about the priesthood, which is that of *discipleship*. It is within this perspective of *pilgrimage,* or *discipleship*, that I present the following remarks on,

---

1. Second Vatican Council, Dogmatic Constitution on the Church (*Lumen Gentium*), 21 November 1964; Pastoral Constitution on the Church in the Modern World (*Gaudium et Spes*), 7 December 1965.

"The Gift of the Priestly Vocation," taking as my primary resource the new *Ratio*.[2]

As the Body of Christ, each of us, in our respective capacities, has the task and responsibility to promote and foster vocations to the priesthood. For its part, the Congregation for the Clergy, which is responsible for the Pontifical Work for Priestly Vocations, desires to support and accompany all who are involved in formation, and in doing so

> "gives practical expression to the concern of the Apostolic See for the formation of those called to Holy Orders" and, among its institutional competencies, is to assist "bishops in ensuring that in their Churches vocations to the sacred ministries are fostered with all possible diligence and that students are suitably educated in seminaries and provided with a sound human, spiritual, doctrinal and pastoral formation." (RF 2)

The *Ratio* reflects the desire of Pope Francis to present formation to the priesthood as an ongoing experience of discipleship, since "priests never stop being disciples of Jesus, who follow Him. Sometimes we proceed with celerity, at other times our step is hesitant, we stop and we may even fall, but always staying on the path. Therefore, formation understood as discipleship accompanies the ordained minister his entire life and regards his person as a whole, intellectually, humanly and spiritually."[3]

In order for us to better appreciate what the church intends with the new *Ratio*, we need briefly to view it within its ecclesial context.

I. Ecclesial Context

Throughout its history, and especially in our present age, the church has had to propose to her members, who were called by the

---

2. Congregation for the Clergy, *The Gift of the Priestly Vocation: Ratio Fundamentalis Institutionis Sacerdotalis* (London: CTS Publications, 2017).

3. Cf. Pope Francis, Address to the Plenary of the Congregation for the Clergy, 3 October 2014.

Lord to share in his Priesthood, a "serious journey of formation" in order for these "'uncut diamonds,' to be formed both patiently and carefully, respecting the conscience of the individual, so that they may shine among the People of God" (RF Intro. 1).

The journey of formation today is vastly different to that addressed in the *Ratio Fundamentalis Institutionis Sacerdotalis*, in 1970. More than thirty years ago, the Congregation for Catholic Education, which was competent for seminaries up until 2013, prior to becoming the competence of the Congregation for the Clergy, sought to amend the *Ratio* above all by updating the footnotes in light of the promulgation of the Code of Canon Law on 25 January 1983. Since then we have had various contributions to the theme of formation from both the universal church and from Conferences of Bishops and individual particular churches. We have especially had the contributions of recent pontiffs: John Paul II and his monumental post-synodal apostolic exhortation *Pastores Dabo Vobis* (25 March 1992); Benedict XVI, who gave us the apostolic letter issued Motu Proprio *Ministrorum Institutio* (16 January 2013); and Francis, whose encouragement, rich Magisterium, suggestions and constant personal example gave rise to the present document.

The *Ratio*, therefore, must not be viewed as a collection of abstract ideas about the priestly vocation but, rather, as a living and organic work that reflects the real-life experience of priests in this third millennium. Priests are called to be *configured* to Christ, the Good Shepherd, who, in his love and mercy, goes out to the peripheries to seek out the lost sheep and lead them home. *Discipleship*, which is at the heart of priestly identity, cannot be switched off; it cannot be limited to specific working hours like 9 to 5, with weekends free. No. Discipleship lasts an entire lifetime, a *pilgrimage* as it were, because the priest is a permanent disciple "whom the Lord has called to 'stay with Him' (cf. Mk 3:14), to follow Him, and to become a missionary of the Gospel" (RF 61). With these preliminary remarks, let us now examine some of the fundamental elements of priestly vocation expounded in the *Ratio*.

II. Fundamental Elements of the Priestly Vocation

A preliminary question that we can ask ourselves is this: Why do we place so much emphasis and give such high esteem to priestly vocations? The primary reason for this is that "ecclesial vocations are manifestations of the immeasurable riches of Christ" (RF 11).

1. Gratitude

Before all else, we must give gratitude to God for the gift of a priestly vocation. On the occasion of his Golden Jubilee to the priesthood, Pope St. John Paul II wrote the following beautiful words:

> I cannot end these reflections, in the year of my Golden Jubilee as a priest, without expressing to the Lord of the harvest my deepest gratitude for the gift of a vocation, for the grace of priesthood, for priestly vocations throughout the world. I do this in union with all the Bishops, who share the same concern for vocations and experience the same joy when their number increases. Thanks be to God, a certain crisis of priestly vocations in the Church is gradually being overcome. Each new priest brings with him a special blessing: "Blessed is he who comes in the name of the Lord." For in every priest it is Christ himself who comes.[4]

2. Prayer

As we give thanks to God for the gift of the vocation to ministerial priesthood, which arises in various circumstances and at different stages of human life, such as in childhood, in adolescence and in adulthood (RF 11), we must continue to pray for such vocations. The *Ratio* highlights this as follows:

---

4. John Paul II, *Gift and Mystery: On the Fiftieth Anniversary of My Priestly Ordination* (New York: Image, 1999), 98–99.

It is the mission of the Church "to care for the birth, discernment and fostering of vocations, particularly those to the priesthood."[5] Welcoming the voice of Christ, who asks all of us to pray the Lord of the harvest to send labourers into his harvest (cf. Mt 9:38; Lk 10:2), the Church dedicates particular attention to vocations to the consecrated life and to the priesthood. (RF 13)

Personal and communal prayer for vocations is encouraged in the new *Ratio*. Evidently, in praying for and encouraging vocations, we do so "not just for one's own Diocese or country, but also for the benefit of other particular Churches, according to the needs of the Universal Church" (RF 14). Finally, the Lord gave Ireland an opportunity to avail of extraordinary graces, especially for the promotion of vocations to the priesthood, in the *World Meeting of Families* held in Ireland in 2018.

3. Adequate Pastoral Care of Vocations

As the Lord, in his mercy, calls forth vocations to the priesthood, it is vitally important to respond adequately to his generosity by means of attentive pastoral care of vocations. This involves recognizing and accompanying the response that is made to the interior call of the Lord, by fostering the growth of the human and spiritual qualities of the person, and evaluating the authenticity of his motives. The church recognizes here the importance, in each particular church, of suitable institutions for the support and discernment of vocations to the ministerial priesthood, such as the Minor Seminary[6] and other similar institutions[7] (RF 17). Accompaniment of one who feels called

---

5. John Paul II, Post-Synodal Apostolic Exhortation *Pastores Dabo Vobis*, n. 34: *AAS* 84 (1992), 713.

6. Cf. *Optatam Totius*, n. 3: *AAS* 58 (1966), 715–716; *Pastores Dabo Vobis*, n. 63: *AAS* 84 (1992), 768–769.

7. C.I.C., can. 234, 1; cf. also *Apostolorum Successores*, n. 86: *Enchiridion Vaticanum* 22 (2006), 1770–1772.

to the priesthood is imperative, as one discerns the "signs of a vocation" (RF 19). Those involved in the early discernment period have a fundamental role in verifying their suitability as candidates for seminary (spiritual, physical, psychological, moral and intellectual).

Constitutive elements of the spiritual life of the candidate for priesthood must be encouraged, especially the importance of Eucharistic Adoration, *lectio divina*, the Liturgy of the Hours, regular confession, spiritual direction, retreats, the rosary and other Marian and pious devotions practiced daily, the purpose of which is to sanctify the candidate and all who form part of the seminary family.

One further element that deserves mention here concerns the intellectual life of the candidate. The young person should receive the education required by his own country for entrance to university and should seek to obtain state-recognised academic qualifications, which will also allow him the freedom and the possibility of choosing another state of life, if it were to transpire that he was not called to the priesthood.

Now that I have given a brief overview of some of the fundamental elements of the priestly vocation, let us take a closer look at the *raison d'être* of formation itself, and the decisive role of formators.

III. Formation and Agents of Formation

1. Initial Formation

The *Ratio* presents formation, understood as one unbroken missionary journey of discipleship, in two principal moments: initial formation in the Seminary and ongoing formation in priestly life (RF 54). There are four stages into which initial formation can be divided, and these are: the *propaedeutic stage*, the *stage of philosophical studies* (or *discipleship stage*), the *stage of theological studies* (or *configuration stage*), and the *stage of vocational synthesis*. The completion of these stages by the seminarian does not earn him the right to ordination. As the *Ratio* states: "one should not arrive 'automatically' at the priesthood merely by reason of having followed a series of pre-established stages in chronological order and set out beforehand, independently of the actual progress that has been achieved in overall integral maturity" (RF 58).

The period of formation is a privileged time in the life of the seminarian that requires of him to be open to the work of the Holy Spirit and to the guidance of the formation team (RF 28).

Let us take a brief look at each of the four stages of formation.

a. The *propaedeutic stage*. We are all too aware of the current cultural and secular climate in which we live, especially in Western Europe, and particularly in Ireland. Experience has shown us the urgent need to dedicate a period of time to preparation of an introductory nature, prior to commencing a program for priestly formation.

> The propaedeutic stage is an indispensable phase of formation with its own specific character. Its principal objective is to provide a solid basis for the spiritual life and to nurture a greater self-awareness for personal growth. In order to launch and develop their spiritual life, it will be necessary to lead seminarians to prayer by way of the sacramental life; the Liturgy of the Hours; familiarity with the Word of God, which is to be considered the soul and guide of the journey; silence; mental prayer; and spiritual reading. Moreover, this time is an ideal opportunity to acquire an initial and overall familiarity with Christian doctrine by studying the *Catechism of the Catholic Church* and by developing the dynamic of self-giving through experiences in the parish setting and charitable works. Finally, if necessary, the propaedeutic stage can help to make up for anything that is missing in their general education. (RF 59)

I take this opportunity to encourage those involved in setting up a propaedeutic period in Ireland to proceed with enthusiasm and dedication.

b. The *stage of philosophical studies* (or *discipleship stage*). Upon entering into seminary, the seminarian begins a more defined journey of discipleship. He "is the one whom the Lord has called to 'stay with Him' (cf. Mk 3:14), to follow Him, and to become a missionary of the Gospel . . . living a deep relationship with Jesus" (RF 61).

During this initial phase of the seminarian's formation

> all possible efforts are expended to root the seminarian in the *sequela Christi*, listening to His Word, keeping it in his heart and putting it into practice. . . . Special attention is given to the human dimension, in harmony with spiritual growth. . . . For priestly formation the importance of human formation cannot be sufficiently emphasised. Indeed, the holiness of a priest is built upon it and depends, in large part, upon the authenticity and maturity of his humanity. (RF 63)

All effort is made to help the seminarian overcome all kinds of individualism, and to foster the sincere gift of self, opening him to generous dedication to others, aided by an ever-maturing prayer life. It is recommended that this period not be less than two years in duration in order for the seminarian to acquire the necessary knowledge of philosophy and of the human sciences (RF 66).

c. The *stage of theological studies* (or *configuration stage*). We call this stage of formation the configuration stage, oriented towards the conferral of Holy Orders, because at the conclusion of "the so-called discipleship stage, formation then concentrates on the configuration of the seminarian to Christ, Shepherd and Servant, so that, united to Him, he can make his life a gift of self to others" (RF 68). During the period of theological studies, the spiritual formation proper to the priest becomes the focus, whereby the seminarian is invited to grow "in the likeness of the Good Shepherd, who knows his sheep, gives his life for them and seeks out the ones that have wandered from the fold (cf. Jn 10:14-17)" (RF 71).

It is during this stage also that the ministries of lector and acolyte will be conferred upon seminarians, according to the maturing of each individual candidate. If the seminarian or the formation team decide, at the end of theological studies, that ordination should not be sought, the journey of formation should be interrupted; if found worthy and willing however, the candidate will be called upon by the church to petition for ordination to the diaconate, thereby entering the clerical state and receiving incardination.

d. *The stage of vocational synthesis*. Upon completion of his formation in seminary, the candidate enters upon that final stage between departure from the seminary, having been ordained a deacon, and his priestly ordination, the times of which must be respected.[8] Bishops, in dialogue with the formation team, must ensure that the deacon is placed with exemplary models of priestly life to inspire, support and guide him. It is during this period also that the candidate is asked to declare freely, consciously and definitively his intention to be a priest, having received diaconal ordination[9] (RF 74).

2. Ongoing Formation

Departure from seminary does not mean departure from formation, since the formation process in the life of the priest is ongoing, within a process of gradual configuration to Christ, where the priest is constantly called to inner growth[10]; after ordination to the priesthood his ongoing formation continues within the family of the presbyterate. "It belongs to the Bishop, with the help of his assistants, to lead priests into the dynamic of ongoing formation" (RF 79), which must not be understood in terms of a mere "updating" in cultural and spiritual matters, relative to the initial formation in the seminary, but, rather, as we read in the *Ratio*:

> *Ongoing* formation is an indispensable requirement in the life of every priest and in his exercise of the priestly ministry. In fact, the

---

8. Cf. C.I.C., cann. 1031, 1 and 1032, 2.
9. Cf. *Optatam Totius*, n. 12: *AAS* 58 (1966), 721.
10. Cf. Francis, Address to the Plenary of the Congregation for the Clergy, 3 October 2014: *L'Osservatore Romano* 226 (4 October 2014), 8.

interior attitude of the priest must be distinguished by an ongoing openness to the will of God, following the example of Christ. This implies a continuous conversion of heart, the capacity to see one's life and its events in the light of faith and, above all, of pastoral charity, by way of a total gift of self to the Church, according to the design of God. (RF 56)

In ongoing formation in the life of the priest, we recall that, "the heart and form of the priest's ongoing formation is pastoral charity"[11] (RF 80).

Each bishop must take special care of his priests, and one way in which this is done is by the promotion of ongoing formation in his diocese, "by a priest or group of priests, specifically prepared for it and officially appointed to assist in ongoing formation" (RF 82). In his turn, "the priest is called to cultivate his missionary zeal, exercising his pastoral responsibility with humility as an authoritative leader, teacher of the Word and minister of the sacraments, practising his spiritual fatherhood fruitfully. Consequently, future priests should be educated so that they do not become prey to 'clericalism,' nor yield to the temptation of modelling their lives on the search for popular consensus" (RF 33).

The life and ministry of the priest will never be devoid of challenges, either from within or without, such as the experience of one's own weakness, the risk of thinking of oneself simply as a dispenser of sacred things, the challenge of contemporary culture, the allure of power and riches, the challenge of celibacy and the veracity of one's total dedication to ministry, to name but a few. The *Ratio* recommends several means of giving concrete expression to sacramental fraternity, which should be encouraged from the time of initial formation, such as fraternal meetings, spiritual direction and confession, retreats, a common table, a common life and priestly associations (RF 88).

---

11. *Pastores Dabo Vobis*, n. 70: *AAS* 84 (1992), 781.

3. Agents of Formation

Those who comprise the team of formators are many and varied (bishop, presbyterate, professors, families, parish community, associations, and so on), with special emphasis being given to the seminary formation team. We read:

> The community of formators is made up of priests who are chosen for it and well-prepared, commissioned to work in the delicate mission of priestly formation. It is necessary that there are formators assigned exclusively to this task, so that they can dedicate themselves completely to it. Thus, they should live in the Seminary. The community of formators ought to meet regularly with the Rector to pray, to plan the life of the Seminary and to assess periodically the growth of the seminarians. (RF 132)

As with all the seminary staff, those who are chosen as formators should exemplify the virtues of priestly identity and thereby inspire, by their priestly witness, those entrusted to their care. Evidently, "each formator should be possessed of human, spiritual, pastoral and professional abilities and resources, so as to provide the right kind of accompaniment that is balanced and respectful of the freedom and the conscience of the other person, and that will help him in his human and spiritual growth" (RF 49). "In the process of formation, it is necessary that the seminarian should know himself and let himself be known, relating to the formators with sincerity and transparency"[12] (RF 45), in an indispensable spirit of "mutual trust"[13] (RF 47).

---

12. Cf. Francis, *Address to Seminarians and Novices from Various Countries of the World on the Occasion of the Year of Faith* (6 July 2013): *Insegnamenti* I/2 (2013), 9.

13. Cf. *Guidelines for the Use of Psychology in the Admission and Formation of Candidates for the Priesthood*, n. 12: *Enchiridion Vaticanum* 25 (2011), 1273–1277.

Ideally, I would like to address each person or group involved in the formation of seminarians; however, I shall limit myself to the following remarks.

a. The Bishop and the Trustees. "It is the Bishop who is primarily responsible for admission to the Seminary and formation for the priesthood. This responsibility is expressed in the choice of Rector and of the members of the community of formators, in the preparation and approval of the Statutes, the Programme of Formation and the Rule of Life"[14] (RF 128).

One of the truly painful aspects of our work at the Congregation for the Clergy is the processing of dispensations from holy orders. This work enables us, however, to observe that many of the difficulties in the life of the priest were already present during his time in Seminary, but they were not sufficiently addressed. With respect to the role of the bishop, allow me to underline the importance of the bishop establishing "a trustful dialogue with seminarians, so as to enable them to be sincere and open. Indeed, 'the diocesan bishop or, for an interdiocesan seminary, the bishops involved, are to visit the seminary frequently, to watch over the formation of their own students as well as the philosophical and theological instruction taught in the seminary, and to keep themselves informed about the vocation, character, piety, and progress of the students, especially with a view to the conferral of sacred ordination"[15] (RF 128).

Having an invested interest in the seminary and especially in his own candidate(s), the bishop and the trustees, should "be diligently attentive not to exercise [their] authority in such a way as to undermine the Rector and the other formators in the discernment of the vocations of the candidates and their adequate preparation. Rather, [they] 'should maintain frequent personal contact with those in charge of the seminary, placing [their] trust in them, so as to en-

---

14. Cf. C.I.C., cann. 242–243.
15. C.I.C., can. 259, 2.

courage them in their task and to foster among them a spirit of full harmony, communion and cooperation' "[16] (RF 128).

Lastly, let me say that the bishop, along with the seminary formation team, "should always keep in mind that, for the good of the Church, pastoral charity, at all levels of responsibility, is not manifested by admitting whomsoever to the Seminary, but by offering well thought out vocational guidance and a sound process of formation" (RF 128).

b. The Presbyterate. The influence that priests have had on vocations to the priesthood has been well documented over the centuries. That said, lest we become complacent, and no doubt we have, "each priest must be aware of his own responsibility regarding the formation of seminarians. In particular Pastors [parochus], and in general every priest who receives a seminarian for a pastoral placement, ought to work generously with the community of Seminary formators, by open and concrete dialogue" (RF 129).

c. The Seminarians. The seminarian is "the protagonist of his own formation, . . . and is called to a journey of ongoing growth in the human, spiritual, intellectual and pastoral areas, taking into account his own personal and family background" (RF 130). "One must always keep in mind that the seminarian first—and later the priest—*'is a necessary and irreplaceable agent in his own formation'* "[17] (RF 53).

The pastoral care of the faithful demands that the priest has a solid formation and an interior maturity, which must be nurtured during his seminary formation. By centring his life on communion with the Lord, the future priest "will be helped to recognise and correct 'spiritual worldliness': obsession with personal appearances, a presumed theological or disciplinary certainty, narcissism and authoritarianism, the attempt to dominate others, a merely external and ostentatious

---

16. *Apostolorum Successores*, n. 89: *Enchiridion Vaticanum* 22 (2006), 1780.
17. *Pastores Dabo Vobis*, n. 69: *AAS* 84 (1992), 778.

preoccupation with the liturgy, vainglory, individualism, the inability to listen to others, and every form of careerism"[18] (RF 42).

d. The Rector. What is required of the rector? "The Rector is to be a priest distinguished by prudence, wisdom and balance, someone highly competent, who coordinates the educational endeavour in the governance of the Seminary. With fraternal charity, he will establish a profound and loyal cooperation with the other formators" (RF 134).

The first responsibility of the rector is care towards his formation team, which requires of him to meet regularly with his colleagues and to listen to them. The rector remains also in dialogue with the bishops, especially those directly involved with the seminary. Another important function of the rector is to assist in the elaboration of a program of "integrated formation," also called the formation itinerary, and of promoting its practical application, in a way that respects the different stages and the pedagogical journey set out therein.

It also falls within the remit of the rector to delegate various competencies to his formation team, such as the coordinators of human, intellectual, spiritual and pastoral formation, all of whom work closely together for the benefit of the seminarians (RF 137).

e. The Spiritual Director or Spiritual Father. What is required of the spiritual director? "The Bishop shall take care to choose competent and experienced priests for the work of spiritual direction, which is one of the privileged ways of accompanying each seminarian in discerning his vocation. The Spiritual Director, or Spiritual Father, must be a true master of the interior life and of prayer, one who helps the seminarian to welcome the divine calling and to develop a free and generous response" (RF 136).

f. Characteristics of the Formation Team. Among the many characteristics of a formation team, I would like to underline, as a sort of parenthesis, a few that are fundamental in every seminary, namely,

---

18. Cf. *Evangelii Gaudium*, nn. 93-97: *AAS* 105 (2013), 1059–1061.

Eucharistic concelebration, spiritual direction, confession, a common table, fraternal correction and trustful collaboration.

g. The Professors. What is required of professors? "Seminary professors are to be appointed by the Bishop or, in the case of interdiocesan Seminaries, by the Bishops concerned, having consulted the Rector and the professors, if this is deemed appropriate. . . . Professors and seminarians are called to adhere with complete fidelity to the Word of God, committed to writing in the Scriptures, handed on in Tradition, and authentically interpreted by the Magisterium. They are to acquire a living sense of the Tradition from the works of the Fathers and Doctors of the Church, whom the Church holds in high esteem" (RF 140).

h. The Specialists. The involvement of experts of various disciplines plays an important role in priestly formation. The *Ratio* states:

> During formation for the priesthood, the presence and contribution of experts in certain disciplines is helpful, owing to their professional abilities and for the support they can give, where particular situations call for it (RF 146). . . . In the field of psychology, this contribution is valuable both for the formators and for the seminarians principally in two areas: in the assessment of personality, expressing an opinion as to the psychological health of the candidate; and in therapeutic accompaniment, in order to shed light on any problems that may emerge and to assist in growth in human maturity"[19] (RF 147).

i. Those in Consecrated Life and the Laity. In any given community of believers, there is a wide variety of charisms, which the future priest will be called to nurture and embolden for the good of the church, thus avoiding the ills of clericalism.

---

19. Cf. *Guidelines for the Use of Psychology in the Admission and Formation of Candidates for the Priesthood*: Enchiridion Vaticanum 25 (2011), 1239–1289.

"The presence of the laity and of consecrated persons in the Seminary is an important point of reference in the formative journey of the candidates. Seminarians should be formed in a proper appreciation of the various charisms to be found in the diocesan community. The priest, in fact, is called to foster a diversity of charisms within the Church" (RF 150).

Of great importance in the process of formation is the fundamental role of women.

"The presence of women in the Seminary journey of formation has its own formative significance. They can be found as specialists, on the teaching staff, within the apostolate, within families, and in service to the community. Their presence also helps to instil a recognition of how men and women complement one another. Often, women are numerically greater among those whom the priest will serve, and with whom he will work in the pastoral ministry. They offer an edifying example of humility, generosity and selfless service"[20] (RF 151).

Conclusion

On 6 November, you celebrated the beautiful and all-important celebration that was the feast of All the Saints of Ireland, which recalled those noble and heroic Irish men and women who persevered in faith, love and fidelity to the Lord during their earthly pilgrimage as his disciples. In the Office of Readings that day, you would have prayed the following from the *Letters of the Popes to the Irish*:

"You have been chosen by the Lord in these last and most calamitous times to renew the pattern of your Church as it was in the beginning. Give yourselves to good works, spend your time in prayer, do nothing contrary to the Catholic religion or to the integrity of

---

20. Cf. *Pastores Dabo Vobis*, n. 66: *AAS* 84 (1992), 772–774; John Paul II, Post-Synodal Apostolic Exhortation *Christifideles Laici* (30 December 1988), nn. 49 and 51: *AAS* 81 (1989), 487–489 and 491–496.

that faith you are proud that your ancestors received from this Holy See. You pride yourselves that your ancestors were men so devoted to God that because of this Ireland won the title of Island of Saints. Show then that you are worthy to be their descendants."

In the concluding prayer at Vespers, that same day, you prayed, and I conclude: "we rejoice to be their countrymen on earth; may we merit to be their fellow-citizens in heaven."

Chapter Three

Priestly Formation after *Pastores Dabo Vobis*

Katarina Schuth, OSF

Ever since Pope St. John Paul II issued *Pastores Dabo Vobis* (PDV) in 1992,[1] the document has had profound influence on seminaries around the world. Seminary leaders have used it as a guidepost for reviewing and revising their programs and structures, so twenty-five years later it is timely to examine "Priestly Formation after *Pastores Dabo Vobis*." In this chapter, the first of three parts shows the relationship between important seminary documents and PDV, with focus on the pivotal *Optatam Totius* (OT), the Vatican II Decree on Priestly Training. The second part deals with the most noteworthy changes generated in seminaries in recent years, especially those derived from PDV. The third part addresses partially developed areas of seminary formation that correlate with the spirit of PDV but are in need of further attention and explication, taking into account the current ecclesial, social, and cultural context.

---

1. John Paul II, Post-Synodal Apostolic Exhortation *Pastores Dabo Vobis*, 25 March 1992.

Only infrequently in its long history has the church published comprehensive documents on seminaries. At the dawn of Vatican II, the existing seminary system was based largely on the Council of Trent's 1563 *Decree on Seminaries*.[2] The council fathers promulgated *Optatam Totius* in 1965; in 1970 the Sacred Congregation for Catholic Education issued the *Ratio Fundamentalis Institutionis Sacerdotalis*, an expanded interpretation of OT. The publication of PDV in 1992 served as a welcome update and was the first major universal seminary document released since 1970. Other contributions to the development of seminary formation in the intervening years were the "Programs of Priestly Formation," prepared by many national bishops' conferences for seminaries under their jurisdiction. In 2016, the Congregation for the Clergy published the new *Ratio Fundamentalis Institutionis Sacerdotalis*.[3]

Part I. Influence on and Relationship of *Optatam Totius* to *Pastores Dabo Vobis*

Of the seven sections in *Optatam Totius*, five pertain directly to seminary formation and the other two are closely related to formation, namely, fostering vocations and ongoing formation, all of which are also addressed in PDV. This chapter begins by identifying each of the main themes of OT and then describing their impact on the

---

2. At the end of the twenty-third session of the Council of Trent in 1563, the council issued its Decree on Seminaries, which "represented a major change in seminary training in terms of its reform of the diverse and inconsistent types of formation for ordination that had prevailed globally over the centuries" (Maryanne Confoy, *Religious Life and Priesthood: Perfectae Caritatis, Optatam Totius, Presbyterorum Ordinis* [Mahwah, NJ: Paulist Press, 2008], 212). The decree ratified an organized approach to seminary formation that lasted for over four centuries.

3. Congregation for the Clergy, *The Gift of the Priestly Vocation: Ratio Fundamentalis Institutionis Sacerdotalis* (London: CTS Publications, 2017).

development of PDV.[4] The introduction to OT emphasized the "extreme importance of priestly training" because its desire for "renewal of the whole church depends to a great extent on the ministry of its priests." PDV elaborated on God's promise that the people will never be without shepherds and so the formation of future priests requires "constant updating of their pastoral commitment." Therefore, it "is considered by the Church one of the most demanding and important tasks for the future of the evangelization of humanity" (PDV 2).

OT I: The Responsibility of Each Nation and Region to Develop Its Own Priestly Formation Program (OT 1)

In its first section, OT directed episcopal conferences to adapt their programs of priestly formation to local circumstances. The council fathers recognized the necessity of considering the "particular circumstances and times" of each place so that the principles of formation would be in harmony with their pastoral needs.

In PDV chapter 1,[5] Pope St. John Paul II wrote in response to the concerns of the 1990 Synod of Bishops, which insisted on having priestly formation updated and contextualized. As prescribed in OT I, PDV considered the circumstances of the present day and determined that this new document would guide the updating of national programs. The pope expected bishops to analyze their local situations as they pertained to "the great variety of socio-cultural and ecclesial circumstances in different countries" (PDV 5).

---

4. The order of topics is different in each document. This presentation follows the order of the OT themes and relates sections of PDV to them. Although PDV is comprised of six chapters—all related to seminaries, chap. 5 (nos. 42–69), "The Formation of Candidates for the Priesthood," has garnered the most attention of seminary personnel.

5. See John Paul II, *Pastores Dabo Vobis*, chap. 1: "Chosen from Among Men: The Challenges Facing Priestly Formation," nos. 5–10.

OT II: The Urgent Fostering of Vocations (OT 2–3)

The second section of OT advocated in strongest terms the urgent need to foster vocations through prayer, penance, preaching, catechetical instruction, and use of social media. It recommended the development of the seeds of vocations in minor seminaries and other special institutes under the direction of superiors and in cooperation with parents. Already at this time, the document recognized as critical the decline of vocations in Europe, and the same situation was to follow within the decade in the United States and other countries.

In PDV chapter 4, and briefly in chapter 1,[6] Pope St. John Paul II addressed the topic of vocations at length. In 1990, the decline in vocations had become a more severe and universal problem. This change prompted the pope to devote attention to societal values in consumer cultures that contradicted the value of a priestly vocation (PDV 5). The negative effect of secular values on young people in their choice of vocation was significant (PDV 8–9). Later, in chapter 4, the pope treated the concern more fully, repudiating the notion that a priestly vocation is a burden and reclaiming it as a gift from God, urgently needed by the church. PDV addressed the topic of vocation in its entirety, both in historical and contemporary terms (PDV 34–41).

OT III: The Setting Up of Major Seminaries (OT 4–7)

Since the promulgation of OT, almost all seminaries repeated verbatim the initial sentences of this section, underlining the fact that major seminaries are necessary for priestly formation: "Here the entire training of the students should be oriented to the formation of true shepherds of souls after the model of our Lord Jesus Christ, teacher, priest and shepherd" (OT 4). Already at this point, OT declared that all forms of training must have a pastoral end.

Toward that goal, OT affirmed the ordering of spiritual, intellectual, and disciplinary areas to the pastoral dimension. Specifically,

---

6. John Paul II, *Pastores Dabo Vobis*, chap. 1, nos. 1–5, and chap. 4, "Come and See: Priestly Vocation in the Church's Pastoral Work," nos. 34–41.

seminarians should be prepared: to make available to the faithful the ministry of the revealed word of God, expressed clearly and revealed by example; the ministry of worship and sanctification, carried out in sacred liturgical celebrations; and the ministry of the parish, making Christ present to the faithful (OT 4).

Formation was designed to help candidates become the servants of all, that they might win over all the more (cf. 1 Cor 9:19). The council fathers reminded the bishops that the success of training depended on the careful selection and testing of students. Moreover, to attain these outcomes, qualified administrators and teachers with pastoral experience, who exemplified a life of faith and service, were to form a close-knit community and "work zealously and harmoniously together, faithfully obedient to the authority of the bishop" (OT 4). Pastoral effectiveness was envisioned as the end of all formation.

In PDV, the title itself, *Pastores Dabo Vobis*, established connection with OT's overall objectives related to major seminaries. The introduction, " 'I will give you shepherds after my own heart' (Jer. 3:15)," replicated the message of OT as it pointed to the importance of the pastoral focus in priestly formation (PDV 1). Two longer sections in chapter 5 described the rationale for the educational format.[7] In "The Setting of Priestly Formation," the seminary was defined as a place and a period in life, and above all as an educational community in progress. Modeled after the experience of the apostles, it was to unite the members with Jesus as the center of an ecclesial community (PDV 60).[8]

---

7. In addition to the brief reference in the introduction of *Pastores Dabo Vobis*, the parallel discussion about setting up seminaries is found in chap. 5, pt. 2, nos. 60–64, "The Setting of Priestly Formation," and pt. 3, nos. 65–69, "The Agents of Priestly Formation."

8. While OT mentioned the importance of careful selection and testing of students, PDV discussed the topic at greater length. It described the selection of suitable candidates in two places: under "Gospel Discernment," chap. 1, no. 10, and especially in "The Vocational Dialogue: Divine Initiative and Human Response," chap. 4, nos. 36–37.

"The Agents of Priestly Formation" explained who constituted the essential facilitators of formation, recognizing the role of five entities: bishops, seminaries, professors, communities of origin, and candidates (PDV 65). The bishop was the first representative in priestly formation in that he symbolized the local church.[9] The seminary, as an educational community, was related integrally to the leaders, that is, "the seminary is built around the various people involved in formation: the rector, the spiritual father or spiritual director, the superiors and professors." In accord with the bishop, they were to be exemplary models who filled different roles in various ways (PDV 66). Teachers had the duty to remain in communion with others and cooperate with all involved in formation. Their character was to reflect generosity, humility, and enthusiasm, as well as deep faith and love of the church (PDV 67). The family of origin, the parish community, and other associations all influenced and contributed to the formation of seminarians by broadening their perspective (PDV 68). Finally, guided by the Holy Spirit, seminarians were charged with ultimate responsibility for their own formation.

OT IV: The Careful Development of Spiritual Training, Including Celibacy (OT 8–12)

The fourth section of OT focused on spiritual training, of which celibacy was a major component. It also introduced the concept of integration. "The spiritual training should be closely connected with the doctrinal and pastoral, and, with the special help of the spiritual director, should be imparted in such a way that the students might learn to live in an intimate and unceasing union with the Father through His Son Jesus Christ in the Holy Spirit" (OT 8). Spiritual formation programs were expected to incorporate the findings of psychology and pedagogy (OT 11).

---

9. The role of religious superiors is comparable to bishops, but PDV concentrated on diocesan seminaries.

Formators had the duty of offering seminarians a balanced view of celibacy, aware of the burdens they would be undertaking in living a celibate life and concealing from them no problem of the priestly life. At the same time, though, they were not to be consumed by the notion of the danger of choosing this path (OT 9). Rather, their spiritual life was to be conformed to strengthening their pastoral work, as professors created an environment permeated by virtues that prepared seminarians for priesthood. OT emphasized the essential attribute of being "saturated with the mystery of the Church" and "totally of service to God and to the pastoral ministry." The pattern of seminary life was intended to initiate candidates into the life of a priest by teaching them self-mastery that would enable them "to work together harmoniously with their fellows and with the laity" (OT 11).[10]

In PDV, Pope St. John Paul II expanded considerably the deliberations on spiritual formation and celibacy and he introduced the concept of "human formation," which incorporated those topics.[11] Human formation was intended to serve as the foundation of all formation. This passage connected it with priestly ministry: "In order that his ministry may be humanly as credible and acceptable as possible, it is important that the priest should mold his human personality in such a way that it becomes a bridge and not an obstacle for others in their meeting with Jesus Christ the Redeemer of humanity" (PDV 43).

PDV addressed other topics of spiritual training, including the evangelical counsels, in which it related celibacy to the spiritual life

---

10. Since human formation was not yet a separate dimension, elements of its later content were partially embedded in spiritual formation in OT, including especially the importance of self-reflection and celibacy.

11. In John Paul II, *Pastores Dabo Vobis*, chap. 3, "The Spiritual Life of the Priest," nos. 19–33, these topics are stressed. Chapter 5, "Human Formation: The Basis of All Priestly Formation," 43–44, treated affective maturity and its relationship to celibacy, and "Spiritual Formation: In Communion with God and in Search of Christ," 45–50, discussed celibacy at length.

of priests (PDV 29). More specifically, it connected spiritual formation with affective maturity (PDV 49).[12] PDV underscored the intent to maintain the law of celibacy and explained its importance in ministry; it also prescribed careful preparation so that seminarians would be able to live a celibate life under present social and cultural circumstances (PDV 50). Spiritual formation was explained more broadly as the process of attending to the development of a deeper relationship and communion with God. Deemed essential were the Eucharist, the sacrament of penance, and prayer through meditating on Sacred Scripture. "The life of intimacy with God, prayer and contemplation, is intended to lead to a life of service to the people of God, offered with pastoral charity" (PDV 45–48).

OT V: The Revision of Ecclesiastical Studies (OT 13–18)

The council fathers determined to require vigorous intellectual formation. As a condition to begin ecclesiastical studies, candidates were to be prepared in humanistic and scientific training. Philosophy, both historical and contemporary, was to take into account the "knowledge of man, of the world and of God" (*Ratio* [RF] 159). Theological studies, too, were to connect with the whole history of the human race and the modern world. Incorporating Sacred Scripture, ecclesiastical studies were to cover a wide range of theological subjects, with emphasis on dogmatic and moral courses, and sacred liturgy. The subjects were to be interrelated and integrated with spiritual and pastoral formation.

In PDV, "Intellectual Formation" gave details about ecclesiastical studies, noting that OT had required "a vast updating of the teaching

---

12. In *The Inner Life of Priests*, the authors offer a basic psychological definition of affective maturity: "the ability to know what one feels, express those feelings, and manage them appropriately through the psychological phases and/or stages from adolescence into adulthood." Gerard J. McGlone and Len Sperry, *The Inner Life of Priests* (Collegeville, MN: Liturgical Press, 2012), 85.

of the philosophical and especially theological disciplines in seminaries" (PDV 56).[13] The need for updating was associated with concerns about certain contemporary problems that raised difficulties, tensions, and confusion within the life of the church. PDV noted that the relationship between statements issued by the magisterium and theological discussion "does not always take the shape it ought to have, that is, within a framework of cooperation" and "the relationship between high scientific standards in theology and its pastoral aim" may be at odds; the two characteristics of theology should not be opposed to each other but should "work together, from different angles, in favor of a more complete 'understanding of the faith'" (PDV 55). Moreover, seminary leaders were "to oppose firmly the tendency to play down the seriousness of studies and the commitment to them" (PDV 56).

OT VI: The Promotion of Strictly Pastoral Training (OT 19–20)

Since the council fathers saw the value of expanding the opportunities for pastoral formation, they believed it was necessary to break from the isolation of seminary life. This stance reinforced the initial discussion of the ultimate purpose of seminary formation as preparing seminarians pastorally (OT III). They were "to learn the art of exercising the apostolate not only theoretically but also practically, and to be able to act both on their own responsibility and in harmonious conjunction with others" (OT 20). Pastoral work was to permeate their course of studies and to be carried out during vacations in their own local circumstances, using practical projects to enhance their skill in pastoral work.

PDV affirmed the principle that formation has a fundamentally pastoral character.[14] It stated that the goal of pastoral formation was

---

13. See John Paul II, *Pastores Dabo Vobis*, chap. 5, "Intellectual Formation: Understanding the Faith," nos. 51–56.

14. In John Paul II, *Pastores Dabo Vobis*, chap. 5 covers "Pastoral Formation: Communion with the Charity of Jesus Christ the Good Shepherd," nos. 57–59.

to seek "really and truly to initiate the candidate into the sensitivity of being a shepherd." Seminarians were to learn to carry out pastoral work with a community spirit, in cooperation with the different members of the church (PDV 59). They were to learn to take conscious and mature assumption of responsibilities, grow in the habit of evaluating problems and establishing priorities, and to look for solutions according to the demands of pastoral work (PDV 58).[15]

OT VII: Training to Be Achieved after the Course of Studies (OT 21)

OT concluded with the topic of ongoing formation, which rounds out the entire process of a lifetime of priestly formation. It noted that ongoing formation was essential for younger clergy, who should attend meetings and pursue studies that keep them up with changing circumstances of contemporary society. Moreover, they should gain familiarity with the spiritual, intellectual, and pastoral aspects of their priestly life as it is being lived. In conclusion, the council fathers acknowledged that the work they did in this document was begun by the Council of Trent. Recognizing the disagreements and the compromises necessary to arrive at the final document, they expressed hope that the bishops would receive these norms willingly.

PDV also devoted considerable attention to ongoing formation.[16] Because of rapid changes in the social and cultural conditions, and because of the new evangelization, which was deemed an essential and pressing task of the church (PDV 70), ongoing formation was prescribed for growth in the path toward maturity and in the exercise

---

15. See John Paul II, *Pastores Dabo Vobis*, "Configuration to Christ, the Head and Shepherd, and Pastoral Charity," no. 23, on pastoral charity; "Seek, Follow, Abide," no. 34 on pastoral work; and "Ongoing Formation," especially nos. 70–71 and 80. PDV references the "pastoral" concept 194 times.

16. In John Paul II, *Pastores Dabo Vobis*, chap. 6, see "I Remind You to Rekindle the Gift of God That Is Within You: The Ongoing Formation of Priests," nos. 70–81.

of priestly ministry. PDV concluded by reminding faculty and administrators that they must realize that "the hope of the church and the salvation of souls are committed to them" (PDV 82).

In summary, the common themes of OT and PDV are many, and a clear progression in interpretation is evident in the twenty-seven years between them. Among the many shared concerns are the necessity of integrating all aspects of formation and the centrality of pastoral and spiritual training, including emphasis on celibacy. Moreover, both documents accentuated the importance of connecting philosophical and theological studies with the modern world and of highlighting Sacred Scripture and the sacred liturgy.

Part II. Noteworthy Changes Implemented since *Pastores Dabo Vobis*

In response to the directives of Pope St. John Paul II in PDV, three pronounced changes were prominent on the agendas of seminary leaders. These topics have not necessarily been dealt with completely, but they do represent notable steps forward: Development of Human Formation Programs; Expansion of Pastoral Experiences through Field Education in Parishes and Other Settings; and a Sharper Focus on Priestly Life and Ministry. The human formation dimension was absent in previous programs, and though it was incorporated in some measure under spiritual formation, it received insufficient attention. Pastoral training had not moved far enough beyond the OT directive concerning the "isolation of the seminary," so pastoral faculty expanded programs and opportunities for seminarians to engage in enriched courses and broader field experiences. The sharper focus on priestly life and ministry arose from the need to concentrate on ministries that only priests could provide. Additionally, some bishops were concerned that seminaries focused insufficiently on the meaning of priesthood as they expanded their missions to include lay ministry students.

A. Development of Human Formation Programs

Since human formation represented a new approach, its addition as a separate dimension required the most substantial development. The rationale for the new program was sparked by rapid cultural changes felt almost everywhere, such as the breakdown of family systems, the weakening of religious practice, and the challenges of technology. As formators launched into the creation and implementation of programs, they identified characteristics that would "foster the growth of a man who will be an apt instrument of Christ's grace in his priesthood, one who takes seriously celibacy, obedience, and simplicity of life" (PPF 76).[17] The goal was to help seminarians grow in emotional maturity, become men of integrity, and develop a moral conscience and moral behavior. A strong emphasis on the role of celibacy resulted in a presentation of the topic in a more persuasive manner than ever before (PPF, esp. 77–79). It aimed at enhancing affective maturity, making it possible to live a true and responsible love, based on valued friendships and priestly fraternity.

Leadership responsibility was most often assigned to a "director of human formation," except when, less preferably, the department was combined with spiritual formation. The director was to be exemplary in his personal maturity, pastoral experience, and appreciation of the psychological and human sciences (PPF 325). As for the structure of programs, a group setting was usual, but almost always included individual guidance as well. The level of the student determined the content, allowing for gradual growth and development.

The 2016 *Ratio*, as previous documents, states that human formation is the foundation of all priestly formation, designed to promote

---

17. The US bishops responded to the directives of PDV in their national *Ratio*, titled *The Program of Priestly Formation*. The United States Conference of Catholic Bishops (USCCB) published the fifth edition in 2005; completion of the sixth edition is projected for 2020. Citations for PPF in this chapter refer to the fifth edition.

the integral growth of the person and the integration of all its dimensions. It names three areas for development: physical, which means an interest in health, nutrition, physical activity, and rest; psychological, which focuses on the constitution of a stable personality, characterized by emotional balance, self-control, and a well-integrated sexuality; and moral, which is connected to the requirement that the individual arrive gradually at a well-formed conscience (RF 94).

As faculties continue to evaluate the efficacy of human formation programs, they take into account the virtues and qualities associated with adult male development expected of priesthood candidates. They review formation policies and processes related to celibacy and sexuality with heightened attention because of sexual abuse by clergy. Seminarians are encouraged to establish mature adult relationships with men and women, peers and older adults. These requirements are aimed at producing what PDV calls ministry that is "as humanly credible and acceptable as possible" (PDV 43).

B. Expansion of Pastoral Experiences:
Field Education in Parishes and in Other Settings

During the past two decades, seminaries made concerted efforts to enhance their pastoral classes and experiences. The impetus came first from OT, and then PDV reinforced the concept. In all aspects, formation programs foster a fundamentally pastoral character, preparing people for ministry of word, worship, and sanctification. The image of shepherd is highlighted, with the caveat that candidates must learn to minister with sensitivity by developing the habit of evaluating problems and finding solutions based on honest motivations of faith and according to the theological demands inherent in pastoral work (PDV 57–58).

To improve the pastoral readiness of candidates, in recent years seminary leaders made available a wider variety of practical pastoral experiences with activities that are multifaceted and focused on future ministry. The purpose is to encourage an open, ecumenical, and collaborative attitude, with a sense of responsibility for initiating and completing tasks and prioritizing those most closely associated with priestly ministry. Seminarians are to cultivate flexibility of spirit, availability, and zeal.

The 2016 *Ratio* affirms these directions and urges seminarians to become men of communion by acquiring the inner freedom to serve, to see the work of God in the hearts and lives of the people, and to see themselves as leaders (RF 119). The *Ratio* specifies: "The call to be pastors of the People of God requires a formation that makes future priests experts in the art of pastoral discernment" (RF 120). This ability implies that the candidate develop a compassionate, respectful, prudent, and serene outlook. It includes a capacity to listen deeply to real situations, to be capable of good judgement in making choices and decisions, and to be free from the temptation to abstraction, to self-promotion, to excessive self-assurance and aloofness (RF 120). The *Ratio* adds that the study of pastoral theology should be upgraded by using the contributions of psychology, pedagogy, and sociology (RF 122). Faculty are continually assessing programs to be certain that they match the changing demographics and spiritual needs of church members living in a radically pluralistic world.

C. Sharper Focus on Priestly Life and Ministry

Several factors contributed to a more intense focus on priestly life and ministry in seminaries. Because of the declining number of priests, seminarians need to be ready to pastor larger parishes and/or several parishes. This shift affects all aspects of priestly life; for example, most priests will live alone and serve with lay ecclesial ministers rather than with other priests. Human and spiritual formation takes into account their ability to cooperate and understand what is necessary to ensure their personal well-being.

In addition to practical realities, regional documents and Vatican visitations of seminaries resulted in other recommendations for seminaries to intensify instruction on the primary responsibilities of developing spiritual initiatives, engaging in community building, and exercising pastoral administration. The US bishops added requirements related to the proclamation of the Word, with emphasis on homiletics, and on effective public ministry through attainment of skills for communicating the mysteries of faith in clear and readily comprehensible language, on using media appropriately, and on considering the social context when planning ministerial undertakings (PPF 239).

The new *Ratio* reinforces these perceptions.[18] In its description of the intellectual dimension, it insists that seminarians acquire solid competence in philosophy and theology, along with a more general educational preparation. This formation should enable them to proclaim the gospel message to the people of their own day in a way that is credible and understandable and makes it possible for them to enter into fruitful dialogue with the contemporary world (RF 116).

Greater focus on priestly life and ministry has strengthened formation programs by concentrating on a clearer sense of priestly identity. Some seminary leaders judge the singular focus on priestly formation less positively for two reasons: Lay ecclesial ministry students who are enrolled and appropriately engaged with seminarians provide an effective means of promoting collaboration. Moreover, the tuition gained from enrollment of lay ecclesial ministry students offers financial support to seminaries, many of which have a relatively small number of seminarians.

---

18. Congregation for the Clergy, *The Gift of the Priestly Vocation: Ratio Fundamentalis Institutionis Sacerdotalis* (London: CTS Publications, 2017). *Ratio* provides the rationale for integrating all dimensions of formation: "The concept of integral formation is of the greatest importance, since it is the whole person, with all that he is and all that he possesses, who will be at the Lord's service in the Christian community. . . . It is necessary to adopt an integrated pedagogical model in order to reach this objective: a journey that allows the formative community to cooperate with the action of the Holy Spirit, ensuring a proper balance between the different dimensions of formation" (RF 92).

Part III. Areas for Further Development in Seminary Formation

Given the directives of PDV and the twenty-five intervening years, several underdeveloped areas of priestly formation persist. For the most part these challenges involve the spiritual and personal backgrounds of candidates and their readiness to address the state of the church and secular society. Thus, the first matter concerns the evaluation of current admissions standards and processes. The other two topics are related mainly to intellectual and pastoral formation: the call for seminarians to acquire a more comprehensive and balanced view of the church and her members and to develop a more thorough understanding of the impact of secular society on religious practice. Although seminaries have made some progress, each of these topics demands more attention.

A. Admission Standards and Practices

The first essential task for seminaries is to evaluate admissions standards. The backgrounds, attitudes, and behaviors of seminarians have tremendous effects on the seminary community and later, when they are ordained, on the church overall. When PDV was promulgated, awareness of widespread sexual abuse by clergy was only beginning to be comprehended, so the pope did not directly address the problem. The document did describe key characteristics expected of seminarians, such as: "a right intention, a sufficient degree of human maturity, a sufficiently broad knowledge of the doctrine of the faith, some introduction into the methods of prayer and behaviour in conformity with Christian tradition" (PDV 62). Admissions standards were to account for the deep diversities that existed among the individual candidates in each diocese and in different regions and countries.

The painful consequences of incomplete or ineffectual vetting of candidates is now well known. In the United States, the fifth edition of PPF provided a lengthy description of the Admissions Process (PPF 34–41) and the required Norms for Admission (PPF 42–67). Different from previous generations, those seeking admission by

2005 represented a more heterogeneous population than before, with diversity in religious backgrounds, personal gifts, levels of maturity, and cultural experience (PPF 38). The Bishops' Committee on Priestly Formation responded to the difficulties suffered from the sexual abuse crisis of 2002 by offering voluntary visitation of seminaries. These reports asked for clearer criteria for admissions, a more precise determination of how to use the results of psychological testing, and assurance that the integration of celibacy formation was evident through entire programs.

Other areas concerning admissions have yet to be fully developed. Some vocations directors are inexperienced, biased, or predisposed and sometimes fail to provide objective evaluations or to inquire adequately about behavior that is indicative of sexual impropriety and lack of emotional control. They may not seek references and documentation that address the general readiness of candidates nor provide clarity and completeness of sexual and psychological history. Finally, to ensure proper discernment, improved processes involving the right number of qualified persons are necessary. The goal of admissions standards is to admit admirable candidates and prevent the admission of those who might cause damage to individuals and the church.

B. Acquire a Balanced View of the Church and Her Members as They Actually Exist

To provide for adequate ministry in the future, more thorough knowledge of the church as it exists presently is essential wherever in the world seminarians will be ministering once ordained. Faculty need to reflect on how well their course materials and field placement experiences address contemporary conditions by interacting with those who have authority and responsibility for ministry in the dioceses/places of ministry of their candidates. Changing dynamics affecting ministry are numerous, among them the disposition of the universal church, the strength of Catholic identity and church attendance, knowledge of whether or not polarization is a factor in the parish, and the strengths and shortcomings of staffing for various types of ministry.

Analysis of the diocesan and parish population also facilitates understanding. To be relevant to the lives of parishioners, those who minister need to translate church teachings into language that is intelligible and meaningful. Pope Francis put it this way: "A preacher has to contemplate the word, but he also has to contemplate his people . . . 'actual people . . . using their language, their signs and symbols . . . answering the questions they ask' " (EG 154).[19] Faculty may need opportunities to improve their knowledge and skills through education about pastoral topics that have not been part of their specialized academic backgrounds. They can interact with peers and others who share the task of seminary education to learn approaches to pastoral situations that enable authentic collaboration and mutual appreciation among those who minister.

Seminarians must be familiar with factual information about the church that will enable them to do their own social analysis. On the parish level, priests need to recognize and appreciate the characteristics of those with whom and for whom they minister. Knowledge about the strength of Catholic identity and the liturgical practices and preferences of parishioners will help them appropriately focus their ministry. Relationships among long-term and new parishioners may reveal whether or not polarization is present, how to deal with inequities in poverty and wealth, and address differences in educational backgrounds. In most parishes, but especially those directly affected by clergy sexual abuse, priests need to acknowledge and be sensitive to the anger and disappointment of parishioners. Priests

---

19. Francis, Apostolic Exhortation The Joy of the Gospel (*Evangelii Gaudium* [EG]), 24 November 2013, http://w2.vatican.va/content/francesco/en/apost_exhortations/documents/papa-francesco_esortazione-ap_20131124_evangelii-gaudium.html.

and lay ministers who can address these issues are much more likely to be able to build a vibrant faith community.

C. Develop a Thorough Understanding of the Impact of Secular Society and Culture

Due in part to the intrusion of the materialistic values of secular culture, those who minister must grasp the impact of these societal pressures, discern how they affect the faith life of Catholics, and determine how to respond. Values found at both macro and micro levels are pervasive. On the macro level, influences are expansive: globalization, immigration, multicultural diversities, and heightened racial, ethnic, and social tensions. Besides that, politics and economic policies often cause widespread poverty and inequity, all of which cause concern for the church. On the micro level, the invasive presence of technology and media along with the rise of scientific knowledge and influence contribute to the breakdown of societal supports for religion.

A critical question to ponder is what has driven so many Catholics from the faith of their birth, especially those of the millennial generation. Based on surveys of young adults (ages 18–35) in the United States, reasons for leaving the church are numerous, but several stand out: science and reason triumph over belief in the transcendent, they no longer believe in the teachings of the church, and families are not particularly religious. The result is that younger generations have not been catechized nor have they grown up in communities of practicing Catholics. In recent years, possibly the greatest deterrent is the clergy sexual abuse scandal, which some studies indicate is responsible for disaffiliation of a third of Catholics from the church.

The difficulties and opportunities created by these factors require focused reflection by seminarians during theological studies and later as priests. Those who exercise priestly ministry need to discover, with parishioners, new possibilities for service and involvement that will build up the entire faith community. Priests have yet to learn more about involving groups and individuals in issues of social justice, which can lead parishioners to engage in opportunities to work together for the good of the whole. Such concrete actions appeal to many parishioners, but especially younger members whose identity as Catholics is often weak.

Conclusion

The goal of this chapter was to examine the expectations of the church regarding seminary formation as expressed in *Optatam Totius* and elaborated on in *Pastores Dabo Vobis*. The purpose of these documents was to recommend practices that more effectively prepare men for priestly ministry so that they are ready to advance the spread of the Gospel completely and faithfully. Deeper insight into the functions of the local church and the impact of secularization requires examining current practices without being self-justifying or self-protective about present practices; rather, they need to ascertain what needs emphasis and make necessary adjustments.

Pope Francis calls attention to the kind of church demanded in these times: one that goes forth to those on the periphery with open doors to all those outside its confines, the poor, the marginalized, the neglected, those without faith, the seekers among the young and the nobodies of this world (EG 20–24). He speaks of cultural challenges (EG 61–67) such as secularism, individualism, and globalization that affect our ability to inculturate the faith, especially in professional, scientific and academic circles (EG 68–70). In the same document, he offers advice that applies to all pastoral formation programs: a priest must be prepared "to contemplate his people . . . 'actual people . . . using their language, their signs and symbols . . . answering the questions they ask'" (EG 154). Seminaries have achieved many of the goals of formation for priests who will serve well in the modern world. Others remain to be fulfilled.

Chapter Four

A Reflection on the Qualities of Candidates Entering Seminary and the Formation Implications

Christopher Jamison, OSB

My experience of candidates for the priesthood comes from my time as a religious superior admitting candidates for the monastic life as well as starting the Compass discernment program that has had some 100 people participate over the past twelve years. More recently I have had the privilege of leading the National Office for Vocation (NOV), an office of the Catholic Bishops' Conference of England and Wales (CBCEW). The work at NOV has included getting to know diocesan vocation directors, seminary rectors and seminarians. I have also been a vocation guide to several people recently as part of our national vocation guides scheme.

But I am not a diocesan priest, so let me make explicit the understanding of diocesan priesthood that will underlie what I say. I will take as my starting point this insight from *Pastores Dabo Vobis*: "the internal principle, the force which animates and guides the spiritual life of the priest is pastoral charity, a participation in Jesus Christ's own pastoral charity, a gift freely bestowed by the Holy Spirit" (PDV 23). I take pastoral charity to be *the* charism of the diocesan priest.

So who are those aspiring to receive and live out this charism in England and Wales today? I emphasise England and Wales because that is the place I know best. As director of NOV, I participated in the conferences of the European Vocations Service and could see that the vocational situation varied from country to country, especially in the former Communist countries of Central and Eastern Europe. However, youth culture is an increasingly global culture and so some of what I say will apply elsewhere.

In Part One I will look at young people in general. I will do this by looking at the religious context of Britain today and at the Preparatory Document for the General Assembly of the Synod of Bishops held in Rome in October 2018. Then in Part Two, the longest part, I will look at the ecclesial and spiritual qualities of candidates, bringing together the secular qualities described in Part One with the specific aspirations of Catholic men entering seminary, their strengths and their weaknesses. Finally, in Part Three, I will consider some of their distinctive formation needs.

1. What Can We Say about Young People in General?

The first thing to note is that they stay young for longer, if by young we mean not yet committed to an adult state of life. The average age for marriage in England and Wales in 2014 was 37 for men and 34.6 for women (all marriage, not just Catholic marriage). This is reflected in the average age for men entering seminary, which in 2016 was 35. Up until about thirty years ago, these average ages of marriage and entry to seminary would have been a full ten years younger, mid-twenties rather than mid-thirties. This means people live through a new phase of life sometimes called emerging adulthood. This is the group known as "young adults," and they have lived as independent, uncommitted people for ten years or more. This independence and this lack of commitment is the first secular quality to note.

So the research I will present will focus on people in that emerging adult age group, people in their twenties. The first piece of research comes from the British Social Attitudes Survey 2014, which tells us that among British youth aged 18–24, 65 percent are not affiliated with any religion. So two-thirds of young people are disaffiliated from religion. But the same survey tells us that among this young group, those who are affiliated to a religion are more likely to practice their faith than the older age group who identify as affiliated to a religion. This means that among this irreligious generation, those who are religious are religious by intention not by inheritance. Even more so, our seminary candidates; they are people who have had to choose faith quite explicitly and are not impressed by half-hearted faith.

Taking these general trends in society, at this point we can describe our candidates as independent men with a faith that comes from strong conviction.

Next, let's look at what the Preparatory Document of the synod has to say about the young, by which they mean those aged 16 to 29. Alongside this, I will also refer to the survey of that age group undertaken by CBCEW as part of our research to answer that document's questions.[1] More than 3,000 people aged 16 to 29 took part, and NOV helped to analyse the data and write the report in collaboration with our Home Mission Office. This report was published in February 2018.[2]

The Preparatory Document identifies three areas of contemporary culture that impact strongly on young people. First, the rapidly changing world which the document identifies as "the main characteristic of contemporary societies and culture." Our survey illustrates the impact of this on young lives. 41 percent are worried about whether they will achieve anything in life, and 20 percent said they have mental health problems. The second aspect of culture impacting the young is that

---

1. At the end of the Preparatory Document, the Office of the Synod asked each Bishops Conference to answer a set of questions. These answers then influenced the synod's Working Document, published in June 2018.

2. This report is available via www.cpo.org.uk/product.aspx?prod=V5569BT.

our new generations experience a major disjunction between their world and that of their parents and educators.

As Pope Francis said, this is not just an era of change; this is a change of era. The religious disaffiliation described earlier is an example of this, as is the huge rise in the age of marriage. I would add that with this delay in marriage, full sexual activity before marriage is now the publicly acceptable norm and I suspect that few will enter seminary without such experience. I think this is a major issue in the formation of celibate men.

This new generation also has new ways of belonging and participation. The demise of accepted classic norms in many areas of life, ranging from music to morality, means that people invent their own lives as they wish; this "turn to the subject" that has characterized modernity means that today the world to which a person belongs is created by himself or herself and not received. Young people belong to their friends and sometimes their families but not to institutions and communities. They lack personal and institutional points of reference other than friends and family. As we move towards a hyperconnected generation, the world of social media has become an alternative to the fellowship previously offered by churches, trade unions and neighborhoods.

In this context, the third cultural feature noted by the Preparatory Document is the way young people make choices. "Tomorrow I choose this, but tomorrow I will see" is how the document characterizes this provisional choosing. The document notes that for many young people, life is precarious and so it is hard to make long-term choices. As well as economic exclusion, some young people experience discrimination of all kinds. They are unable to choose because they are excluded.

In spite of all these difficulties, when our survey asked the 3,000 respondents to describe their lives overall, 61 percent used a positive descriptor such as good or great. This is a generation full of hope who see that in an era of change, traditional structures break down and young people can achieve great things quickly. For them, life is relationships not structures or careers or institutions.

So let's put all this together to describe the generation from which our seminary candidates are drawn. The people currently aged in their twenties are self-sufficient, and a small minority have strong religious faith. They are worried about their uncertain future and some have mental health problems. They are disconnected from large institutions and rely on friendship groups online and off-line. While they find it hard to make lifelong choices, most feel empowered to create a better future.

From my experience, those general qualities are also found among candidates for seminary. If that describes their social situation, let's now look in more detail at their ecclesial and spiritual situation.

2. The Ecclesial and Spiritual Life of Seminary Candidates

This generation's strongest ecclesial characteristic is that they love the Catholic Church. They have struggled hard through their youth to choose Catholic faith, and they want a church with a clear identity. Now that identity is varied, ranging from those who love classic liturgy through to those who are socially active with groups such as Young Christian Workers. What unites them is a sense of Catholic identity that is personal, not tribal. Ecumenism is not a priority for them.

Their strongest spiritual characteristic is that they have all been through a process of conversion. For some, this was a moment in time during an Alpha course or at a youth event. For others, a moment when they rediscovered a lost faith of their childhood. For others again, a conversion from another church to the Catholic church. In England and Wales, almost all seminarians are converts or reverts, or at least they can tell you when they found faith. Essentially, candidates have discovered a personal relationship with God and have become disciples open to hearing the Lord's call. Yet the zeal of the convert or revert needs time to mature; how long does it take not simply to become Catholic—how long does it take to *be* Catholic? Many young men who discover Christian faith anew or for the first time think that the only way to deepen their relationship with Christ is to become a priest. That needs testing.

The feature of candidates that is both ecclesial and spiritual is the centrality of the Eucharist in their lives. For candidates, the Mass is truly the source and summit of their faith. And eucharistic devotion plays a large part in their prayer life. It is worth adding that our survey revealed that many self-identified young Catholics still find Mass boring; it is a characteristic of candidates to have grown beyond that. The insight I offer here is that somebody has managed to explain the Mass and engage those who go on to become candidates while most Catholic youth don't get that opportunity.

So this generation of candidates is strongly Catholic, having come to intentional faith during the emerging adult period and they are devoted to the Eucharist. I could add more, but I think those three points are worth highlighting.

Let's now look at the spiritual pitfalls of being a seminarian today, and these will lead clearly to some formation needs. These pitfalls are often expressions in the spiritual life of those qualities of secular culture described earlier.

First, autonomous people who have chosen faith can view their faith as a gift for themselves rather than as a grace to serve those in need. They recognize the priestly charism of pastoral charity in theory, but they may need to learn what Matthew 25 means in practice through formation.

Second, the later date of entering seminary means that losing the autonomy that they have had for a decade or more is difficult. Yet this personal deconstruction is a necessary part of formation. Not a process of humiliation through silly practices but a real spiritual stripping back to basics. This can lead to distress and panic, but if well handled by a formator, it is a key moment of formation. The image I have is of somebody enthusiastically setting off to climb up a mountain pass.

After a while when the way gets hard, the walker questions why he ever agreed to do this. Then after more hard climbing, he wonders if he's going to find the strength to get to the top, and at this point panic can set in. This is when a good companion can accompany the person and encourage him to keep going. When he gets to the top of the pass, the walker sees a beautiful valley lying before him. As he walks down into the valley, he realizes that this new world is why he set out; he could only get there via the hard work of climbing the mountain pass. I suspect that the hard climb of stripping away self-sufficiency is the most necessary and most demanding formation need of seminarians today.

Next, narcissism is a growing quality in our culture, and it is so prevalent that some psychiatrists identify it as a disease; so we shouldn't be surprised to find it in seminary. Yet self-importance can mask a self-loathing that comes from the broken family experiences that are all too common. Self-determination combined with personal fragmentation can be lethal in a candidate. It is from this combination that clericalism emerges: joining this elite cast will solve my problems and give me a strong identity. This can be combined with an unacknowledged desire for a father, into which role an unwitting vocations director can step; and so between candidate and director, an insecure vocation can be manufactured.

This raises the whole area of discernment. There is a new category of young Catholics: those "in discernment." This is a wonderful development in many ways, but it, too, has pitfalls. Some committed young Catholics can experience discernment as a heavy burden. God has a plan for them, but the discerner can't find it. Some can become paralyzed and join our largest religious order, the little brothers and sisters of perpetual discernment. We need to do much more to provide discernment help in a clear way.

It can help to introduce some Thomist rigor here. A Christian has an *inclination* to marriage or to religious life as spiritual goods. But an attraction, as distinct from an inclination, is always to a person or group or people. Such attraction needs to be tested, and a person needs others to help in discovering what truly attracts him or her. Left on his or her own, a young person can experience this discernment as a burden, so the person needs the help of others. I believe the synod and the ensuing apostolic exhortation will ask the local church to become much better at providing this help in parishes. This is a formation need of the local church. The new *Ratio* for priestly formation sees the first two years of seminary as formation in discipleship before a man is called to specifically priestly formation. This discipleship process begins before seminary in the local church.

The final pitfall to note is one for the formators. Most candidates today have great zeal for evangelisation; this enthusiasm reflects the optimistic outlook revealed in the England and Wales youth survey. It also reflects the fact that most candidates are converts/reverts who have discovered rather than inherited a personal faith in the Lord. They are eager to share this newly discovered faith, and maybe this is a pitfall for their formators. Is formation able to engage with this zeal to channel it and form it without extinguishing it?

Using some of the terminology from the *Ratio* for priestly formation, this self-sufficient generation is filled with evangelical zeal but needs to be led through a process of rebirth to become disciples filled with pastoral charity, ready for configuration into the priesthood of Christ.

3. Formation Needs

I want finally to offer three spiritual priorities for formation that I believe address both the reality of the candidates and the reality of the church.

First, induction into communion. The basis of the pastoral charity of the priest is the church as *koinonia*. That love of sacramental communion I noted must become a love of human communion, and that begins with love of the brethren. When an invitation to spend a day with their bishop is ignored by significant numbers of priests, there is something flawed in the communion of the presbyterate. Hopes of serious permanent formation expressed in the new *Ratio* won't happen without this presbyteral communion. An encouraging sign is that many dioceses have discernment groups for men considering the priesthood and these groups are greatly valued by those who participate, a seed of presbyteral communion.

Second, the ability to distinguish the good spirit from the bad spirit. To live a life of communion requires an awareness of the good spirit and bad spirit at work in one's own soul. I use this Ignatian categorisation as shorthand for whatever theology of grace one has and for whatever demonology one espouses. The general point is that the good spirit builds communion and the bad spirit loves to destroy it. A man wanting to live the charism of pastoral charity as a priest must get beyond an examination of conscience for confession; he must regularly within himself "test the spirits" and assess the direction in which his spirit is moving, into closer communion or away from it. It is possible to confuse becoming aligned with a particular group as entering into deeper communion with Christ. Communion with Christ and the church needs to be both Catholic and catholic, not partial. Perhaps most of all a candidate must learn when the bad spirit comes dressed as an angel of light; wise formators can help him make that discernment. Some of the Catholic blogosphere is full of the bad spirit masquerading as enlightenment, and this can have an unhelpful influence on those entering formation.

The third and final priority for this generation of seminarians is to ensure the story in their heads is the story of the Gospel. We all catch ourselves making ourselves into the story in our heads. The daily reading of Scripture in which the star performers are Father, Son and Holy Spirit is the necessary antidote to the bad spirit. Without this deep engagement with the Word of God, the bad spirit can take control and make me the star of my life, which then leads to less and less communion. Vocation directors rightly emphasize that the potential candidate is invited to apply for formation as a priest. The man is called to this formation; he is not entitled to it.

In all of these areas, vocation directors, spiritual directors and other supporters play a vital role. They need to be patient accompaniers, not directive gurus with all the answers. They need to believe that the Holy Spirit is the director of the candidate and that their role is to enable the person in front of them to listen to the Spirit. When confronted by a talented young man with headstrong ideas, it is easy to respond in kind, telling him what's right and wrong, what he should do next and so on. Yet such people need forbearing accompaniment that keeps reflecting what they say so that the candidate begins to hear his own voice in a new way, no longer so self-confident but more open to the Spirit and rooted in the prayer of quiet contemplation. When heard more clearly, that call of the Holy Spirit may be to the priesthood or elsewhere, but it will now be the Spirit, not the candidate, who is setting the direction for the journey.

Let me conclude with a story of a candidate to pull all this together. This immensely able and personable man in his mid-twenties said that God had put into his heart from a young age the idea of being a priest. He was in touch with his vocations director, who asked him to become more involved in parish life in order to live out pastoral charity in practice. The parish priest invited him to help with the pastoral care of the elderly and infirm who were housebound by taking them communion on a weekly basis. He was also asked to help with other parish activities and to receive spiritual direction. At the end of nine months, he showed great generosity of spirit when he said that he had come to realize the nature of his early motivation to be a priest. He had wanted to join a special group by becoming a priest so that he could bestow grace on those in need. Through visiting the sick and spiritual direction, he had come to realize that the sick were blessing him when he visited them and he had learnt to love them with a very genuine affection. He had laid aside a form of clericalism and come to discover the charism of pastoral charity. His story of conversion of heart through visiting the sick shows a love of communion as both the sacrament he gave them and of them as people. He discerned with great honesty that a bad spirit had captured his soul with thoughts of superiority, but through pastoral charity and spiritual direction he shook himself free from that and the grace of true discernment flowed into his life. He is now free to discover if God really is calling him to be a priest. Whether he becomes a priest or not, his journey of discernment is one that illustrates many of the qualities of those entering seminary today and the formation that they need even before they arrive at the seminary door.

Chapter Five

Analogia Ecclesiae—
Models of Priesthood:
Some Implications for Formation

Kevin O'Gorman, SMA

I open with the observation of Kenan B. Osborne about the two major documents of Vatican II that address priesthood and priestly formation—*Presbyterorum Ordinis* and *Optatam Totius:*

> It is essential that both documents be studied through the lens of the primary doctrinal document of Vatican II, *Lumen gentium.* . . . Since a theology of the priest can be understood only in the light of a theology of the Church, and since the formation of priests can be accomplished only in the light of a theology of the Church, the ecclesiology of *Lumen gentium* is foundational. One cannot lose sight of the fact that ecclesiology determines the meaning and role of the ordained person in the Church. The theology of the ordained person does *not* determine ecclesiology.[1]

---

1. Kenan B. Osborne, "Priestly Formation," in Raymond F. Bulman and Frederick J. Parrella, eds., *From Trent to Vatican II: Historical and Theological Investigations* (Oxford: Oxford University Press, 2006), 126–27.

Ecclesiology is thus the initial entry point for understanding the vision of priesthood which underpins the values inherent in the formation of priests. The relationship between church and priesthood is analogical, and I attempt to articulate this through the application of Avery Dulles's models of the church to the priesthood. Originally outlined in five foci for describing the mystery of the church—*institution, mystical communion and herald, servant and sacrament*[2]—Dulles later added a sixth, the church as *community of disciples*.[3] Another—a seventh model of priesthood—is presented, inspired by the writings and witness of Pope Francis—the priest as *man of mercy*. This sevenfold stance is supported by the statement of Daniel Donovan:

> The ordained ministry is a rich and many-sided reality, and there are a variety of legitimate approaches to it. What is important in a period of change is that one be open to, and include in one's understanding of it, as many of its elements and aspects as possible.[4]

This is supported by Dulles himself who, as Donovan declares, "given the variety of models, [he] felt it unwise to attempt to formulate 'a single tight definition of priesthood'."[5] The subtitle of Dulles's original *Models of the Church* is *A Critical Assessment of the Church in All Its Aspects*. Since it is clearly not possible to present a critical assessment of the priesthood in all its aspects here, I hope to analyze the vision of priesthood in terms of the seven models, adducing the key value inherent in each and applying these to formation. In

---

2. See Avery Dulles, *Models of the Church* (Dublin: Gill and Macmillan, 1976).

3. See Avery Dulles, *Models of the Church—Expanded Edition* (New York: Doubleday, 1987), especially chap. 10.

4. Daniel Donovan, *What Are They Saying about the Ministerial Priesthood?* (New York: Paulist Press, 1992), 138.

5. Donovan, 135.

attempting this, I am aware of the caveat contained in the words of William Cosgrave:

> Each model has its own values, though some models are better than others. . . . But no one model is fully adequate on its own and so they should be seen as complementary rather than as opposed to one another, despite real conflict between different models at a variety of points. In addition, in different times and ages different models will appeal and work more satisfactorily. Our age is no exception.[6]

Dulles's first four models can be correlated with the four columns of formation found in *Pastores Dabo Vobis*[7]—the *institutional* intersects with human formation, *mystical communion* with spiritual, *servant* with pastoral and *herald* with intellectual. Daniel J. O'Leary offers a useful summary: "The document balances the priest's life of contemplation with his life of pastoral action, his call to be a shepherd. This balance is found and maintained by the priest, as he strives, in his total humanity, to be 'the living and transparent image of Christ the priest.'"[8]

Institution

"Show me your man and I will show you your God"—is an observation once made by Theophilus of Antioch. For many people, both in parish and public, the priest is their point of contact with the church. He is, in the phrase of Karl Rahner, "an official institution" in the church and involved in effecting its mission statement of evangelisation

---

6. William Cosgrave, "Models of Priesthood Today," *Doctrine and Life* 47 (September 1997): 424.

7. John Paul II, Post-Synodal Apostolic Exhortation *Pastores Dabo Vobis*, 25 March 1992.

8. Daniel J. O'Leary, *New Hearts, New Models—A Spirituality for Priests* (Dublin: The Columba Press, 1997), 28.

which entails—in a word much favored by Pope Francis—*encounter*. Francis says that he never tires of "repeating those words of Benedict XVI which take us to the very heart of the Gospel: 'Being a Christian is not the result of an ethical choice or a lofty idea, but the encounter with an event, a person, which gives life a new horizon and a decisive direction.'"[9] True encounter with others ensures that the priest is not a clerical functionary playing a role. Rahner once wrote that "the priest of the future [present] will depend, in his concrete living, upon the question of whether he is really a man who lives from the heart and center of his own personal existence as one who bears witness to the faith and arouses faith in others."[10] To be this "sign and instrument"[11] of the faith implies the incarnational imperative of human formation for the priesthood. This has two immediate implications. First, the recognition that the key issue and index of this formation is the integrity of the seminarian/priest himself and, second, the realisation that, in the words of Gerald D. Coleman, "human formation is a progressive achievement, a lifelong pilgrimage. Seminarians and priests are always preparing themselves."[12]

Mystical Communion

Dulles's second model—*mystical communion*—balances the institutional with the internal, the individual with the communal. This communion is envisaged within the universal call to holiness

---

9. Francis, Apostolic Exhortation The Joy of the Gospel (*Evangelii Gaudium*) (Dublin: Veritas, 2013) 7.

10. Karl Rahner, "The Point of Departure in Theology for Determining the Nature of the Priestly Office," *Theological Investigations*, vol. 12 (London: Darton, Longman and Todd, 1974), 56–57.

11. Second Vatican Council, Dogmatic Constitution on the Church (*Lumen Gentium*) 1.

12. Gerald D. Coleman, *Catholic Priesthood—Formation and Human Development* (Liguori, MO: Liguori Publications, 2006), 36.

expressed in *Lumen Gentium*. Moreover, paragraph 13 of that document states that "between all the various parts of the church there is a bond of intimate communion whereby spiritual riches . . . are shared" (LG 13). The priest is invited to receive these riches in order that the spiritual and human dimensions of his formation may be integrated, as Paul intimates in his invocation in Ephesians 3:14-19: the purgative way, to "be strengthened in [the] inner being with power"; the illuminative way, "that Christ may dwell in [the] heart through faith"; the unitive way, to "be filled with all the fullness of God." As a minister of *mystical communion*, the priest is called to protect and promote the right of the Christian faithful "to follow their own form of spiritual life so long as it is consonant with the doctrine of the Church," as stated in canon 214 of the Code of Canon Law.[13] An example of this ministry of communion is given in Roberto Morozza della Rocca's description of how Oscar Romero "had personal ties with the Christian Cursillos and with Opus Dei . . . he had good relations with the Neocatechumenal Movement and the Knights of Christ the King, with Marriage Encounter groups and the charismatics; he promoted Marian devotion and the worship of the Sacred Heart."[14] *Mystical communion* gives the lie to any kind of spiritual solipsism or *mé féinism*.[15] Formation for *mystical communion* is, rather, in terms that Romero would have understood (and perhaps used), an option for the faithful and the many forms of spiritual life in the church.

---

13. For a fuller treatment see my "The Right of the Christian Faithful to Spirituality in Canon 214," in Brendan Leahy & Séamus O'Connell, eds., *Having Life in His Name—Living, Thinking and Communicating the Christian Life of Faith* (Dublin: Veritas, 2011), 81–90.

14. Roberto Morozza della Rocca, *Oscar Romero—Prophet of Hope* (London: Darton, Longman and Todd, 2015), 123.

15. This Irish idiom literally means "myself alone" and indicates a principle/practise of privatisation.

Herald

In his *Letters to Priests*, Pope St. John Paul II highlighted the herald model. In 1982 he wrote: "We thank you [Lord] for having likened us to you as ministers of your priesthood . . . not only through the administration of your sacraments, but also, and even before that, through the proclamation of your message of salvation," and in 1986: "you are deeply convinced of the importance of proclaiming the Gospel, which the Second Vatican Council placed in the first rank of the functions of a priest."

The herald model is heavily biblical. Luke presents Jesus in prophetic terms while Mathew ends his gospel of Jesus the teacher in true fashion, telling the eleven to teach all nations to obey "everything that I have commanded you" (28:20). The *Rite of Ordination* tells *ordinandi*: "You must apply your energies to the duty of teaching in the name of Christ, the chief Teacher." These energies embrace exegesis and exploration, explanation and elucidation. To become a herald means first being a hearer, and this must be helped by serious study, a habit developed in the seminary. The study of philosophy, literature and the human sciences deepens human formation while the study of theology dovetails with spiritual formation. The importance of intellectual formation is indicated in a pamphlet produced to raise money for the new Harvard College in 1643: "After God had carried us safe to New England, and we had built our houses, provided necessaries for our livelihood, reared convenient places for God's worship . . . one of the next things we longed for, and looked after was to advance learning and perpetuate it to Posterity; dreading to leave an illiterate Ministry to the Churches, when our present Ministers shall lie in the dust."[16] This concern for posterity was reiterated by Archbishop John Quinn more than twenty years ago: "Certainly we must beware of over-emphasizing the intellectual qualities of the seminarian. It would

---

16. Myron B. Bloy, "Faith Communities in the Academic World," *Cross Currents* 43 (Winter 1993–1994): 443–44.

be equally harmful to the Church to have highly intellectual priests who lack holiness or pastoral sensitivity, who are not really integrated human beings. But I insist: the future of the Church will not be served by the ordination of men who have no intellectual depth and only a superficial theological education."[17]

Servant

"It is striking that even some who clearly have solid doctrinal and spiritual convictions frequently fall into a lifestyle which leads to an attachment to financial security, or to a desire for power or human glory at all cost, rather than giving their lives to others in mission."[18] These words of Pope Francis in The Joy of the Gospel echo the teaching of *Gaudium et Spes* that "the church is not motivated by earthly ambition but is interested in one thing only—to carry on the work of Christ under the guidance of the holy Spirit, who came into the world to bear witness to the truth, to save and not to judge, to serve and not to be served."[19] Together these testify that the human, spiritual, theological models of evangelisation—and therefore of priestly formation—must be viewed and evaluated through the servant model. Translating this into the pastoral program of the seminary means bringing together the three strands stated by the council—witness, wisdom and willingness. Without any of these, pastoral formation is truncated. Pope Francis's words—"giving their lives to others in mission"—are explicated in the exhortation:

---

17. John Quinn, "The Priest of the Future in the Church of the Future," Address to the seminary section of the National Catholic Education Association, 4 April 1994.
18. Francis, *Evangelii Gaudium* 80.
19. Second Vatican Council, Pastoral Constitution on the Church in the Modern World (*Gaudium et Spes*) 3.

> Our commitment does not consist exclusively in activities or programs of promotion and assistance; what the Holy Spirit mobilizes is not an unruly activism, but above all an attentiveness which considers the other "in a certain sense as one with ourselves." This loving attentiveness is the beginning of a true concern for their person which inspires me effectively to seek their good.[20]

"Loving attentiveness" cannot be entirely expressed in an agenda and is not equated with aid. It is the attitude that appreciates others beyond any actuarial assessment and, animated by the Gospel spirit of generosity, acts to alleviate deprivation and distress. The genuineness of this spirit of service will be shown and seen in the course of pastoral formation.

Sacrament

If the models of *institution* and *mystical communion*, *herald* and *servant* are the four cornerstones of priestly ministry, the sacramental is their foundation. Or, to change the metaphor, if they are the cardinal points, the *sacramental* is the compass needle. The key issue in the sacramental model of priesthood is identity. The sacramental synthesizes the institution's visible sign and the herald's voice, seeing the priest as sacrament to be the vehicle, or the vessel. The sacramental synthesizes the intellectual search for wisdom and the servant struggle for solidarity, seeing the priest as sacrament to be the well. Both of these biblical metaphors, the one Pauline, the other Johannine, point beyond to what they bear, Christ the Water of Life. Cardinal Joseph Ratzinger—Pope emeritus Benedict XVI—ended his address at the opening of the 1990 Synod of Bishops on Priestly Formation with words from Pope St. Gregory the Great who wrote of "the rivers of holy men" and "what they pour forth in public as they work and speak,

---

20. Francis, *Evangelii Gaudium* 199.

they draw in secret from the fountain of love."[21] At a summer school on the theme of priesthood in Maynooth nearly fifty years ago, Joseph Ratzinger spoke of "the Christological foundation of the priesthood in the church."[22] This is reinforced by the statement of John O'Donnell that "the priest knows that from the Gospel perspective such a way of life still makes eminent sense, for it has firm Christological roots in Jesus the servant who loved his own and loved them to the end."[23] Reference to roots recalls Paul's "being rooted in Christ" and John's image of the vine and branches which are reminders of the priest's indispensable relation to Christ. These roots entwine the priest as both "man of God" and "man for others," enabling him to bear fruit for the glory of God and the good of others. Thus Colman E. O'Neill wrote that "the abiding sacrament, even more clearly than in the case of baptism, can only be given by the risen Christ who, through it, brings the priest into a permanent relationship with himself in view of his own personal entry into the community in the Eucharist."[24] This iconic and not instrumental understanding of priesthood enfolds the *institutional* model with that of *mystical communion*. Identifying the priest in relational and not functional terms energises the *herald* model with that of *servant*. Initial formation needs to identify the importance of imaginatively integrating the sacramental model of priesthood with these other four.

---

21. Joseph Ratzinger, "The Nature of the Priesthood," in John F. Thornton and Susan B. Varenne, eds., *The Essential Pope Benedict XVI—His Central Writings & Speeches* (New York: HarperSanFrancisco, 2007), 304.

22. Joseph Ratzinger, "Mediator and Minister of Christ," in Gerard Meagher, ed., *Priest: Person and Ministry* (Dublin: Gill and MacMillan, 1970), 62.

23. John O'Donnell, "Priestly Identity and Spirituality," *The Month* (May 1987): 186.

24. Colman E. O'Neill, *Sacramental Realism—A General Theory of the Sacraments* (Dublin: Dominican Publications, 1983), 195.

Disciple

Dulles developed the model of the church as *community of disciples* just over a decade after his original work, drawing "on a passing remark in the first encyclical of Pope St. John Paul II." Dulles's comment that "the theme of discipleship suggests a more modest concept of Church than some others we have mentioned" could be said to apply *a fortiori* to the priesthood. This is contained in the clarification and consolation that he offers: "The disciple is by definition one who has not yet arrived, a learner trying to comprehend strange words and unravel puzzling experiences. He is still on the way to full conversion and blessedness of life. In the life of the church today, that is what most of us feel ourselves to be."[25] As Pope Francis said, "a priest has never 'arrived.' [He] always remain[s] a disciple, a pilgrim on the roads of the Gospel and life, looking out over the threshold of the mystery of God and on the holy land of the people entrusted to him."[26] Mindful that, in the words of Karl Adam, we are "always on the way to Christ,"[27] this description of discipleship delivers an honest self-appraisal for priests, present and future. Moreover, *community of disciples* delivers clericalism its *coup de grâce* without the need for a *coup d'état*! The only control that counts in the Christian life is self-control. James and John were not called to be jihadis or judges, fulminating and calling down fire from heaven, but to follow Jesus on the way to Jerusalem. Linguistic, liturgical and legal terrorism are not part of the church's lexicon of formation for priesthood. As Dulles states, "the sacrament of ordination is rightly understood as an instance of discipleship. . . . Only mature disciples, thoroughly schooled in the

---

25. Dulles, *Models of the Church—Expanded Edition*, 215.

26. Francis, Address to the Plenary of the Congregation for the Clergy, 1 June 2017, https://w2.vatican.va/content/francesco/en/speeches/2017/june/documents/papa-francesco_20170601_congregazione-clero.html.

27. Karl Adam, as quoted in Robert A. Krieg, *Karl Adam: Catholicism in Catholic Culture* (Notre Dame: University of Notre Dame Press, 1992), 153.

ways of the Lord, should be presented for ordination."[28] This model finds strong support in the *Ratio* which states that "the priest-disciple comes from the Christian community and will be sent back to it."[29]

Man of Mercy[30]

In "The Church: Community of Disciples," Dulles commented that "the obligation of every disciple to show mercy and compassion has been recognized throughout the ages."[31] In his address to the joint session of the United States Congress in September 2015, Pope Francis named four Americans, the final one being the (naturalised) Cistercian Thomas Merton. "Mercy within mercy within mercy"[32] is the mantra for Thomas Merton's life both as monk and priest. In his early years in the monastery, Merton was inclined to interpret his vocation as involving himself and God alone. However, in the passage of time and his own passionate interest in the issues of the day, both nationally and internationally, he rejected any residual *contemptus mundi* as he saw the compassion of God in Christ reaching out to cover everyone, to the ends of the earth. Thus John Moses notes that "Merton had changed in his understanding of himself and of contemplation [and] the difference was the degree to which he could now identify with the questions and the pain of the world" and quotes from his *New Seeds of Contemplation* that "contemplation is out of the question for anyone who does not try to cultivate compassion

---

28. Dulles, *Models of the Church—Expanded Edition*, 216–17.

29. Congregation for the Clergy, *The Gift of the Priestly Vocation: Ratio Fundamentalis Institutionis Sacerdotalis* (London: CTS Publications, 2017), intro., 3.

30. For a fuller treatment of this model see my own "The Priest as Man of Mercy," *Doctrine and Life* 66 (September 2016): 23–31.

31. Dulles, *Models of the Church—Expanded Edition*, 221.

32. Thomas Merton, "Epilogue: Fire Watch, July 4, 1952," *The Sign of Jonas* (Dublin: Clonmore and Reynolds), 354.

for other men."[33] Mercy is the golden thread running throughout Merton's writing, gathering together his expanding concern for moral and political issues, manifesting his increasing ecumenical and interreligious exposure. His essay on the parable of the Good Samaritan expounds this *par excellence*.[34] *Mercy* stitches together the solitude and solidarity of Merton's life. Recalling his time as a clerical student in a central London parish, Father Gerry Cleere reported the response of an old man named Peter who was destitute and confused by the question he had asked him about the most important thing for a priest to be: "The sympathy of God."[35] The pathos of the priest as man of mercy is powerfully penned in Oliver Goldsmith's portrayal of the village preacher:

> Unpractis'd he to fawn, or seek for power,
> By doctrines fashion'd to the varying hour;
> Far other aims his heart had learned to prize,
> More skill'd to raise the wretched than to rise.
> His house was known to all the vagrant train,
> He chid their wand'rings, but reliev'd their pain:
> The long-remember'd beggar was his guest,
> Whose beard decscending swept his aged breast;
> The ruin'd spendthrift, now no longer proud,
> Claim'd kindred there, and had his claims allow'd;
> The broken soldier, kindly bade to stay,
> Sat by his fire, and talk'd the night away;
> Wept o'er his wounds, or tales of sorrow done,
> Shoulder'd his crutch, and show'd how fields were won.

---

33. John Moses, *Divine Discontent: The Prophetic Voice of Thomas Merton* (London: Bloomsbury, 2014), 98.

34. Thomas Merton, "The Good Samaritan," in Thomas P. McDonnell, ed., *A Thomas Merton Reader*, rev. ed. (New York: Image Books, 1974), 348–56.

35. Alice Taylor, review of *The Sympathy of God*, Gerry Cleere (Campus Publishing Ltd.: Galway, 1991) in *The Furrow*, 43 (1992): 325.

Pleas'd with his guests, the good man learn'd to glow,
And quite forgot their vices in their woe;
Careless their merits, or their faults to scan,
His pity gave ere charity began.[36]

Under the heading of the "Pastoral Dimension of Formation," the *Ratio* reprises the central metaphor of its predecessor *Pastores Dabo Vobis* in calling the pastor to reflect "the gaze of the Good Shepherd," calling for him to become "a sign of mercy and compassion, witnessing to the motherly face of the Church which, without diminishing the demands of the Gospel truth, avoids making millstones of them, leading rather with compassion and including all."[37] This reflects the mission of the Messiah of mercy who invites those who are weary and are carrying heavy burdens to come to him so that he can give them rest (cf. Matt 11:28). Manifesting the mercy of the Father, Jesus shows the measure of ministry which "will not break a bruised reed / or quench a smoldering wick" (Matt 12:20). This is the prototype of what Pope Francis proposes in *Amoris Laetitia*, "The Logic of Pastoral Mercy."[38] This formation in and for mercy is the foundation for the process of discernment which enables the seminarian and (future) priest to be(come) like the scribe "who has been trained for the kingdom of heaven is like the master of a household who brings out of his treasure what is new and what is old" (Matt 13:52).

Pope Francis has stated that "the centrality of mercy, which for me is Jesus' most important message, has slowly evolved over the years in my work as a priest, as a consequence of my experience as a confessor, and thanks to the many positive and beautiful stories

---

36. Oliver Goldsmith, *The Deserted Village*, in *The English Parnassus* (Oxford: Clarendon, 1940), 228, lines 145–62.
37. Congregation for the Clergy, *Ratio* 120.
38. Francis, The Joy of Love (Dublin: Veritas, 2016) 307–12.

that I have heard."[39] With the emphasis on the mission of mercy as the mainstay of the church's ministry expressed in Pope Francis's concentration on what might be called the "climate of compassion," a mission statement for priestly formation, both initial and ongoing, might be fruitfully formulated along the following lines: to prepare priests who, personally and prayerfully, prophetically and pastorally, are mediators of the mystery of Christ and ministers of his mercy to the pilgrim people of God in the power of the Holy Spirit. This formation would flesh out the final line of the blessing of seminarians given by Pope St. John Paul II at St. Patrick's College, Maynooth, in October 1979, a copy of which hangs in the college sacristy: "Father, raise them up as worthy ministers for your altar and gentle servants of your Gospel. Through them may the compassion of your Son, Jesus Christ, heal the wounds of sin and division."

Conclusion

A major theme of the conference behind this volume, a topic treated in a number of chapters, has been integration. Integration involves the dimensions of priestly formation identified in *Pastores Dabo Vobis*—human and spiritual, intellectual and pastoral—and the stages indicated in the *Ratio*. A "models" approach such as that articulated here advances important insights into the content and course of priestly formation. First, it points to the process of this formation, that is, to the pilgrim journey of the priest as person and the person as priest. Due consideration needs to be taken and given by both formators and candidates to the cultural context of this process. Second, there is no super model that synthesizes or even summarizes the seven models of priesthood here. (Dulles initially indicated this in relation to his seminal statement of the models of the church.) Third,

---

39. Francis, The Name of God Is Mercy (*Pastores Dabo Vobis*) (London: Bluebird, 2016) 3.

while individuals may indicate preference for a particular model at a certain point, that should not exclude the others, seeing them simply as options. The integration of priestly identity involves all of the demands of formation delineated in terms of dimensions and stages in *Pastores Dabo Vobis* and the *Ratio*. This must be insisted upon in programs of priestly formation. A question raised at the conference about the relationship between diocesan and religious priests underscores this point. While monastic and missionary perspectives on the ministerial priesthood may prefer or propose a particular model as primary, this should not be at the price of ostracizing others. The prize or price of formation is witness to the one priesthood of Jesus Christ. Fourth, the task of integration initiated in the seminary does not isolate the seminarian from the people of God, giving him a sense of self-importance. Integration is the ongoing invitation to incarnate as "an official institution" in the church priestly spirituality and study, solidarity and sacramental service with the humility of discipleship and the hallmark of mercy.

Chapter Six

Training for Catholic Priesthood in Ireland Today: Looking Back to Look Forward

Brenda Dolphin, RSM

Introduction

"I will give you shepherds after my own heart, who will feed you with knowledge and understanding" (Jer 3:15). These were the words used by Pope St. John Paul II as he concluded his exhortation *Pastores Dabo Vobis*.[1] They carry the promise that God will always give his people "shepherds"—and not any kind of shepherd, but shepherds after God's own heart. This sustains hope and the recognition that God is always with his people. It is also integral to priestly training and points to its culmination.

---

1. John Paul II, Post-Synodal Apostolic Exhortation *Pastores Dabo Vobis* 82, 25 March 1992, http://w2.vatican.va/content/john-paul-ii/en/apost_exhortations /documents/hf_jp-ii_exh_25031992_pastores-dabo-vobis.html.

Pastores Dabo Vobis and the New Emphasis on Human Formation—Education and Individual Accompaniment

In 1992, the call to place greater emphasis on the human formation of the prospective priest was gaining momentum. With the advent of *Pastores Dabo Vobis*, it was placed on an equal footing with the spiritual, intellectual and pastoral training of the future priest.

In the beginning, the call to more in-depth human preparation was received cautiously: conferences, symposia on human growth and development were added to the seminary curriculum. In particular, the area of affective maturity, the handling of the sexual and emotional areas of living, found its way explicitly into the education of the prospective priest.

Side by side with this educational perspective, the emphasis on the one-to-one accompaniment of the seminarian as a means of enabling him to gradually internalize the values that he proclaimed by the very fact of his choice for priesthood gradually found its place in the formative experience. The one-to-one vocational accompaniment gained entry into the seminary world after clarification of the initial suspicion that it could usurp the place of spiritual direction or that it would interfere with the internal forum of the individual seminarian.

It is generally recognized that a person needs to know himself humanly, his strengths and his limitations, before he can legitimately offer himself to God (in priesthood) or to another person (in marriage). In simple terms, we cannot offer to another person or to God what we do not possess. With this recognition, the pathway to be walked opens more and more clearly and reveals that, side by side with the breathtaking ideal that is priesthood: "I will give [them] shepherds after my own heart," the lived reality points to the law of graduality. This enables the seminarian to learn, slowly but surely, that the balance between the exaltation of the ideal and the "downer" that comes with the recognition of human limitation can be lived in a way that is balanced and which leads in the long run to authentic human, spiritual and pastoral maturity. As the seminarian gradually grows in the conviction of his priestly identity, he simultaneously becomes less reliant on the role or any other external structure.

The Gift of the Priestly Vocation[2]

When we read the *Ratio* today, we find that it, too, describes the priestly ideal very well, as did *Pastores Dabo Vobis*, and all the documents on seminary formation produced by the church.[3] The challenge is as great as the call implies:

- total self-giving/consecration in all aspects of one's person. (A priest may go on holiday but he can never take a holiday from being a priest.)

- single-minded recognition of the value of each individual member of his "flock," especially the weaker one, the one who is inclined to get lost

- loving to the very depth of his being those entrusted to his care

These are lovely words, but the reality of what they are asking is stark and immense. What has been learnt in seminary formation over the past twenty-five years is that growing towards the ideal of priesthood is a lifelong journey. The journey does not proceed in a straight line from the starting point of entry into the seminary to the moment of ordination and beyond; growth in fact, in any area of human development

---

2. Congregation for the Clergy, *The Gift of the Priestly Vocation: Ratio Fundamentalis Institutionis Sacerdotalis* (London: CTS Publications, 2017).

3. Congregation for Catholic Education, *Guidelines for the Use of Psychology in the Admission and Formation of the Candidates for the Priesthood* (Roma: Libreria Editrice Vaticana, 2009). Congregation for Catholic Education, *Basic Norms for Priestly Formation* (Roma: Libreria Editrice Vaticana, 1985). This is just a random sample from the many documents published since Vatican II on various aspects of priestly formation.

moves forward spirally. Oftentimes, it is a case of making three moves forward towards the ideal accompanied by two moves backwards. With a spotlight on human formation, the seminarian learns that in life the human person often regresses; that is, he or she falls back into a less mature mode of behavior, especially in the face of difficult and stress-filled situations. If the seminary environment provides a safe holding space for self-reflection on this "regressive behavior," the result can often be a recouping of personal resources that help him to move forward at ever-deepening levels of being and living.

Respecting the law of gradatuality in human and spiritual growth has also allowed for better understanding about the pace at which each person moves forward through the required stages of formation. In earlier times, all seminarians were expected to move forward at the same pace and each was expected to be ready for the ministries of reader, acolyte, diaconate or ordination at the same time. The emphasis on human formation has allowed seminary formation to be personalized, meaning it is tailored to the growth and development of each individual person moving at his own pace. So, a person is not "disgraced" either in his own eyes or in the eyes of others if he does not arrive at diaconate with the men who started out on the journey with him. It has become more acceptable that each person follows his path of discernment, and while generally people who start the seminary journey together may well arrive at ordination at more or less the same time, it is not precluded that some members of a class, for whatever reason, may take more time than others to reach a particular milestone. This attitude toward the formative discernment process is more realistic and allows the person in formation to really live his experience instead of putting an emphasis on performance.

Women and Seminary Training

The emphasis on human development has also led to an increased number of women being involved in seminary training in the last twenty-five years in comparison to the years before that. This again is something that has brought benefits to a seminary training program as the reciprocal complementarity of the sexes enriches as well as remains integral to human living. Seminarians, who will make a promise of chaste celibacy and will also promise to live in perfect continence for life, must have the possibility to interact with women as adult to adult and relate with them on an equal basis in an open, friendly and mature way from the very beginning of their formation into priesthood. Otherwise, they may find themselves in relational difficulties in later life, either created by inappropriate distance or inappropriate intimacy. As *Pastores Dabo Vobis* says, "affective maturity, which is the result of an education in true and responsible love, is a significant and decisive factor in the formation of candidates to the priesthood" (PDV 43).

The possibility of interacting with women of their own age and outlook is also a very solid means of allowing for priests' growth and development into mature relationships with others. This is an excellent way of building a secure sense of identity both as a man and as a priest. Working on projects, on teams, sharing hobbies, sport and relaxation in the company of women is education in itself for the prospective priest.

Again, if the individual seminarian avails himself of the practice of one-to-one vocational accompaniment, he will be in the position where he is enabled to reflect on ongoing relationships and to notice what is happening within himself in the various encounters. If he is able to learn from this experience of reflective living, it will in turn lead to a deeper discernment of his call and ongoing response to the totality of that call.

Relationships are one of the most important aspects of all human living for everybody: priests and laymen, women and men, young and old. So daily, close interaction with women at various levels—peer, senior and junior to oneself—can only enhance the preparation for a life that will constantly call for engagement with a variety of people.

Any effort that would restrict the place of women in the formation program can only be a backward step.

Formative Experiences

Over the years, the power of the experiential in life has been increasingly recognised. From a formation perspective, the seminarian needs field/learning experiences that:

- will allow him to test himself in substantially different tasks in various social situations—not necessarily nor solely in a confined seminary or parish setting

- challenge him increasingly to move beyond his existing abilities and broaden his skills base in areas of activity in which he has some competence

- afford him a safe place where he can reflect on and explore his reactions in these experiences, integrating them as he recognises his strengths and his failures. This will enable a growing sense of personal and priestly identity.

Aspects of Formation Encouraged in *Pastores Dabo Vobis* but Not Yet Present in Mainstream Seminarian Formation

One of the areas that has been consistently encouraged by the church in seminary formation is the possibility of a propaedeutic year before starting into life in the seminary proper. Pope St. John Paul II endorsed the practice in *Pastores Dabo Vobis* (62) and it is highlighted again in the *Ratio*. The willingness to add an extra year to an already long preparation for priesthood demands foresight and sacrifice, but its importance cannot be underestimated. The one element that unites the men who join the seminary today is the fact that all or at least the majority wish to become diocesan priests. From the perspective of lived spirituality, they come from very differing backgrounds and since they come to the seminary at various ages, with a broad variety of life experiences, the propaedeutic year is a means whereby they can find common ground in their search for a spirituality of diocesan priesthood. Men who intend to be part of a religious congregation, at the outset of their training, experience a period of novitiate together, an experience that is based on the charism of the founder of their congregation and which forms a common bond from which the prospective priests go forward. The seminarian for a diocese has no such common ground unless in some way he can experience a focused and extended period of a common spiritual search with others who are starting the same journey towards the same goal.

The Prospective Priest and the Cultural Milieu within Which He Finds Himself Today

As well as God's promise in the Old Testament, "I will give you shepherds after my own heart" (Jer 3:15), in the New Testament, the shepherd is also the human image that Jesus uses to describe himself: "I am the good shepherd" (John 10:11). Jesus used this image to communicate God's desire for fullness of life for his people and Jesus' own single-minded loving care for those entrusted to him to the point of giving his life for them. The primary focus for the priest and for his formation is the people of God. If the focus of the shepherd is God's people, then the *cultural milieu* into which the new priest must insert himself must be kept to the fore when discussing seminary formation.

The Catholic population in Ireland today has need of well-adjusted, well-educated and especially deeply spiritual and truly holy priests. However, in the collective Irish psyche, the aftermath of the clerical sexual abuse scandals still lingers. This influences how people perceive the priestly ministry today. There are negative perceptions of priestly life and the call to live chaste celibacy. The morale of many good priests has been significantly undermined, which in turn affects how they themselves portray the joy of their ministry. There is, it would seem, an undercurrent of reaction to the relative power wielded by the Catholic Church in Ireland, especially in the last century. This reaction, not always spoken, can effectively neutralise any public statement the priest may legitimately wish to make.

There is in vogue a dismissive attitude towards Christian values coupled with a pervasive humanistic, relativistic, liberal mentality that tends to relegate religion to the private sphere.

There can also be a corresponding reaction within the Catholic Church community to the above, which can lead to extreme entrenched positions that also create tension and discord.

The Catholic Church in Ireland today is very much on the periphery of society in terms of its influence on the daily life of the majority of people. It is not that they reject religion or the church per se, but they see her role in their lives more as an accompanier than as a moral guide. This is not the whole story but is part of the existing reality of the Irish Catholic Church today.

The above raises questions for the kind of formation that is being offered to the prospective priest today as a preparation *for his life tomorrow.*

On a parallel line, since it does not call into question the formation process per se but could undermine it, is the call for "new wineskins" in terms of the contemporary parish structure and the demands that will face the new priest in an increasingly diminishing pool of priests available for service. The existing parish structure will not sustain the life of the newly ordained priest unless something very different is formulated. The question is raised in this context because formation is understood to be lifelong and therefore the transition from life in the seminary to life in a parish needs to have some credible coherence. Questions that need urgent attention are: What are the radical changes of parish structure that are envisaged, and how are they finding their way into the training of the prospective priest?

One of the ways, highlighted in all documents and mentioned once again in the recent *Ratio* (61) is the focus on discipleship.[4] It

---

4. Discipleship is understood here as the integration of the human and the spiritual within the person, thereby enabling the necessary freedom for total self-giving for the people to whom one is sent.

is one of three stages described in the *Ratio,* but in its fundamental essence it encompasses what is necessary for a future priest who must live his priestly life in a context that has few external supports. He needs to be a Catholic and a priest by conviction and not simply by culture.

Freedom and Growth as a Disciple

According to Pope Francis, a shepherd has a heart sufficiently free to set aside his own concerns. The following is one practical way of trying to understand how we can grow into effective freedom as a disciple of Jesus Christ.[5]

Discipleship is our essential vocation as Christians. Belonging to Jesus, loving him, learning from him and responding to him in love are what give meaning to our lives. Discipleship gives us a sense of identity as members of the church, as having a mission in life.

One of the important things that discipleship does is that it keeps the reform of the church to the fore; it saves our theology from becoming too theoretical, too intellectual, and too propositional. Discipleship means we learn theology on our knees.

Von Balthasar, in his book *My Work in Retrospect*, has described discipleship as "effective listening to the one who calls and growth in freedom for the expected response."[6] Effective listening and growth into freedom for living a response to gospel values can be more easily

---

5. Essentially, we are free as human beings to choose among various alternative and possible courses of action. This freedom may be effectively limited because of emotional influences, conscious or unconscious. We are not always effectively free then to make the choices we might wish to make, especially in the area of acting according to Christian self-transcendent values which make demands on human nature.

6. Hans Urs von Balthasar, *My Work in Retrospect* (San Francisco: Ignatius, Communio Books, 1990), 52.

understood if we engage with what Bernard Lonergan described as the "self-corrective process of learning."[7]

In his book *Insight: A Study in Human Understanding* (1957) and later in *Method in Theology* (1972), Lonergan speaks about a normal process of learning in the life of the human person (self-corrective process) whereby we have an experience in life, we reflect on that experience, and we make a judgment about it which leads to a decision and then to a new experience which we reflect on, and so on . . . the understanding being that we learn cumulatively from our experiences of life. By the time Lonergan wrote *Method in Theology* (fifteen years after *Insight*), he could say that the self-corrective process of learning sometimes advances and sometimes is blocked. In other words, he recognized the fact that humanly we do not always learn from our experience in life, we do not always succeed in self-transcendence.[8] We can often know what we ought to do, what is best for us spiritually, humanly, physically, without being actually able do it, because in certain areas of our lives the willingness (usually unconscious) needed to change is lacking, and in these areas we are "effectively unfree." Being effectively free means being free enough interiorly to hear what God is saying to us and what response is expected in a given situation. This capacity to listen effectively or to learn from experience is not something that comes from maturing years (chronological age), or from years spent studying (theology or philosophy or psychology), nor from merely proclaiming gospel values. It has to do with the choices we make in the here and now in day-to-day life that

---

7. Bernard J. Lonergan, *Insight: A Study in Human Understanding* (London: Longman, 1958); *Method in Theology* (London: Darton, Longman and Todd, 1973).

8. Lonergan's Transcendental Method: Conscious intentionality enables the person to advance through a series of questions; from the experience of objects to the effort to understand them; from understanding to the effort to judge truly, from judging to the effort to choose rightly (Lonergan, *Method*, 108). In this way the person transcends himself or herself.

cause an inner harmony or disharmony between the persons we are (seen in daily choices) and the persons we want to be, shown in the values that we proclaim (our desire to grow into being the shepherds God calls us to be).

Discipleship arouses *hope* and *joy*; it also makes great demands on human nature. If we generally make choices in line with our values, even if costly, then we will end up being "cheerful giver[s]" (2 Cor 9:7) and sharing freely what we have received. If our choices generally are for what pleases us and our own comfort, then we can end up seeing discipleship as deprivation and not as a source of freedom.

How Is It Possible to Detect a Lack of Effective Freedom in Living Discipleship?

One of the ways that we can grow into awareness is to watch out for patterns of behavior in ourselves that are repetitive and that do not respond directly to a given situation or which we are incapable of modifying, given changing circumstances.

Some Practical Examples of Ways of Growing into Freedom

One way is to learn to ask ourselves the "further" question and not take at face value spontaneous reasons that come to mind for why we do or don't do something! We can be slow to question our own behaviors in case our security is threatened. By challenging ourselves as to what really might have been behind a spontaneous/regular reaction might help us to refocus and lead to change.

Another way might be a willingness to listen to ourselves as we say "yes . . . but" in response to others and to God because oftentimes the greatest unconscious resistance will be hidden behind our "yes . . . but." A good strategy is to listen to the "recurring but" in our lives and to promptly explore this, preferably with another person such as a spiritual director, an *anam chara* (soul friend), or a vocation counsellor.

Lectio divina has been rediscovered in our time. It is a helpful means (especially for the busy person) to slow down, to learn to savor and to allow the word of God to seep into the very marrow of our souls, and to allow ourselves and especially our actions to be challenged again and again by Jesus' all-embracing love.

Growth in Discipleship Shows Itself in Our Becoming More Like Jesus

Here we take just one example of this configuration. Jesus shows great freedom in the way he lives relationship with others; he always meets the other person where she or he is at, and that takes self-knowledge and self-possession. Some examples include his response to the good thief on the cross (Luke 23:43), or his interaction with the woman from Samaria (John 4:5ff.) or again the encounter between himself and the Syrophoenician woman (Matt 15:21ff.).

Pastoral Synthesis and Priestly Holiness

In the *Ratio*, pastoral synthesis deals with the final stages of the formation experience. On another level and following Hebrews 5, synthesis also has to do with the dispositions of the heart of the priest formed in the image of Jesus Christ, who was gentle and humble of heart. The prospective priest's training must lead him in the same direction: being gentle with his brothers and sisters and accepting who he is before God (humility), nothing more and nothing less.

From a formation perspective, the above is a very cursory description of the essential stages in priestly formation according to the *Ratio*. What is intended here is the highlighting of that interpenetration of the human and the spiritual, the intellectual and the pastoral so that no aspect of the person of the prospective priest is left unattended if he is to grow into full maturity in Jesus Christ, something that is a lifelong project but that needs tending and nurturing all along the way.

For Today the Ratio *Highlights the Importance of Community in the Life of the Seminarian*

The "seminary" of Jesus was not a building but a relationship. For his apostles and disciples, formation is a challenging journey into human and spiritual maturation; a journey into true love. During his life on this earth, Jesus lived in community—first in his family and his hometown of Nazareth where he was well known, and then when he moved on to do what he believed his Father was calling him to do. Many people began to gather around him, fascinated by what he had to say and the way he communicated it, by how he lived, what he said and his obvious power to heal. One of the first things Jesus did after his baptism and time in the desert was to gather a more intimate group of twelve apostles around him, a group that he formed with love and patience. They were a motley group, to be sure, of different ages and ways of thinking and behaving and from varied walks of life, all having one thing in common: when he invited them to follow him, they came to him knowing very little about the path they were going to walk but each in his own way and in his own heart trusted this compelling man. In the company of this small band, Jesus spent the rest of his life. He prayed and ate with these companions; he travelled and rested in their company; he taught and healed; he got angry and he relaxed; he cooked breakfast and he helped pay taxes; he defended his followers and also challenged them. He surprised them and he sought their support. He also suffered betrayal and abandonment at their hands. He opened his heart to them and shared all he had with them. For the group who formed community with Jesus, life was changed forever. Finally, looking at Jesus with his disciples, we notice that it is the community or group that he commissions to go out to the whole word and not an individual. The Christian community as Jesus intended it is a corporate body, widely differentiated internally but with one head, Jesus Christ, and a unity of purpose to share the Good News. Jesus' example is enough to show us how important community life is for the diocesan priest, how necessary is a network of relationships within which he can insert himself and with whom he can interact on a daily basis.

No *Ratio* for formation will have any great effect in the life of the future priest if the priests of his diocese are not willing to study and engage in conversation about its contents and if they are not willing to be mentors to the new priest. Where are our St. John Vianneys today? Where is the priest of Georges Bernanos's *Diary of a Country Priest*?[9] They are there and we all know them. Oftentimes their lives are hidden with Christ in God, but that renders them all the more capable of being mentors to the newer members of the diocesan presbyterate.

Into the Future—Some Questions

There is perennial hope to be found in the wise words of Rilke (1903): "Live the questions now. Perhaps you will then gradually, without noticing it, one distant day live right into the answer."[10]

Many ask the question: Is the seminary setting as we know it today the most suitable means for attaining the goals of initial formation for the diocesan priest and for the world from which he comes and to which he must go? The *Ratio* argues that it is the most suitable for this time. There are situations where the existing seminary context is necessary, for example, in places where the intake into a national seminary can rise to hundreds of candidates in any one year. However, where there is a small group of candidates, might not a smaller locale enable a greater sense of human and interpersonal growth and interaction?

Also, is it possible to envisage a more diverse intake into what we know as the seminary formation process today? Such an intake

---

9. George Bernanos, *The Diary of a Country Priest* (London: Macmillan, 1937).

10. Rainer Maria Rilke, *Letters to a Young Poet*, trans. Reginald Snell (Mineola, NY: Dover, 2002), 21.

might include women as well as men, people preparing for pastoral work and other ministries in parishes, and people preparing for the diaconate as well as those preparing for ordination.

It might also be helpful to consider raising the age limit at which training for the priesthood begins.

Conclusion

The conclusion is a partial quote from a radio lecture delivered by Joseph Ratzinger many years before he was elected pope.

What will the church of the future look like?

> From the crisis of today the Church of tomorrow will emerge—a church that has lost much. She will become small and will have to start afresh more or less from the beginning. She will no longer be able to inhabit many of the edifices she built in prosperity. As the number of her adherents diminishes, so will she lose many of her social privileges. In contrast to an earlier age, she will be seen much more as a voluntary society, entered only by free decision. . . . Undoubtedly, it will discover new forms of ministry and will ordain to the priesthood approved Christians who pursue some profession. In many smaller congregations or in self-contained social groups, pastoral care will normally be provided in this fashion. Alongside this, the full-time ministry of the priesthood will be indispensable as formerly.
>
> The Church will be a more spiritual church, not presuming upon a political mandate. It will be hard-going for the Church, for the process of crystallization and clarification will cost her much valuable energy. It will make her poor and cause her to become the Church of the meek. The process will be all the more arduous, for sectarian narrow-mindedness as well as pompous self-will will have to be shed. . . .
>
> And so it seems certain to me that the Church is facing very hard times . . . but I am equally certain about what will remain at the end: not the Church of the political cult, which is dead already, but

the Church of faith. It may well no longer be the dominant social power to the extent that she was until recently but it will enjoy a fresh blossoming and be seen as man's home where he will find life and hope beyond death.[11]

---

11. Joseph Ratzinger, "Radio Lecture, Christmas 1969," in *Faith and the Future* (San Francisco: Ignatius, 2006), chap. 5.

Chapter Seven

Authenticity in Education for Ministry

Aoife McGrath

Integration is one of the four characteristic elements of priestly formation as developed in *The Gift of the Priestly Vocation: Ratio Fundamentalis Institutionis Sacerdotalis*.[1] It was also the recurring theme or underlying premise of priestly formation that emerged from the papers presented at the Models of Priestly Formation conference, which sought to imagine a process of formation appropriate for the priests of tomorrow. It has its roots in the vision explicitly set out in John Paul II's *Pastores Dabo Vobis*, which specified the coordination

---

1. The other three characteristic elements are as follows: (1) the journey of formation is "one," single journey of "continuous configuration to Christ" (whereby priests participate in Christ's one priesthood and saving mission), but two phases can be identified within this journey, initial and ongoing formation; (2) priestly formation is "grounded in community," such that a vocation must always have as its point of reference a specific portion (or community) within the people of God, where such a vocation is discovered and accepted; and (3) it is "grounded in [a] missionary spirit," since its goal is participation in the one mission of Christ entrusted to the church (Congregation for the Clergy, *The Gift of the Priestly Vocation: Ratio Fundamentalis Institutionis Sacerdotalis* [London: CTS Publications, 2017], intro., sec. 3, par. 1).

and unity of the different areas of formation—human, spiritual, intellectual, and pastoral.[2]

The *Ratio* developed this vision further by emphasizing the integration, or "interior synthesis," of two aspects of the seminarian's humanity—his strengths (understood as talents and gifts molded by God's grace) and his weaknesses (marked as he is by human limitation and frailty); the integration of his personal situation and history into a deep spiritual life; the integration of all aspects of the seminarian's personality or personal life—physical, psychological, sexual, moral, interpersonal/social (especially relationships with women), etc.; the integration of the organic and academic study of philosophy and theology with the exercise of ministry; and the need for a gradual cultural integration if seminarians leave their own country and receive formation elsewhere.[3] The task of formation, in this context, is to help the seminarian to achieve integration "under the influence of the Holy Spirit, in a journey of faith and of gradual and harmonious maturity, avoiding fragmentation, polarisation, excesses, superficiality or partiality."[4]

The premise of integration is so influential in the *Ratio* that educators in a seminary community might consider it the fulcrum on which the formation of the seminarian is balanced. It could be the point of support between, on the one hand, the weight of what preparation for priestly ordination requires of a seminarian (i.e., a complete giving of himself for the service of the people of God, such that the candidate can have within himself the same feelings and attitudes that Christ has towards the church[5]) and, on the other, the effort of

---

2. John Paul II, Post-Synodal Apostolic Exhortation *Pastores Dabo Vobis* (25 March 1992) 57, 71.

3. Congregation for the Clergy, *Ratio* 28–29, 43, 94, 118, 26–27.

4. Congregation for the Clergy, *Ratio* 28.

5. John Paul II, *Pastores Dabo Vobis* 65; Congregation for the Clergy, *Ratio* 39.

the seminarian himself, as an irreplaceable agent in his own formation and protagonist of reaching integral maturity.[6] Educators could provide such support through both pedagogical approaches and their own witness.[7]

The degree of importance given to integration (and its position within the overall process of formation) determines the type of formation the seminarians will receive, the very effectiveness of the whole formation process, the shape and structure of the identity of the seminarian and future priest, and the quality of his future ministry practice. Thus the significance of this premise cannot be overstated:

> The concept of integral formation is of the greatest importance, since it is the whole person, with all that he is and all that he possesses, who will be at the Lord's service in the Christian community. The one called is an "integral subject," namely someone who has been previously chosen to attain a sound interior life, without divisions or contradictions. It is necessary to adopt an integrated pedagogical model in order to reach this objective: a journey that allows the formative community to cooperate with the action of the Holy Spirit, ensuring a proper balance between the different dimensions of formation.[8]

Here, I engage indirectly with the notion of integration and the corresponding need for the seminarian to attain a sound interior life, which makes it necessary for educators within a seminary to adopt an integrated pedagogical model for the education or formation of candidates for the ordained priesthood. I am particularly concerned with

---

6. John Paul II, *Pastores Dabo Vobis* 69, "the actions of the different teachers become truly and fully effective only if the future priest offers his own convinced and heartfelt cooperation to this work of formation"; cf. Congregation for the Clergy, *Ratio* 127.

7. Congregation for the Clergy, *Ratio* 127, 132.

8. Congregation for the Clergy, *Ratio* 92.

a certain challenge to the ministry and life of the priest highlighted in the *Ratio*, namely, the challenge of contemporary culture.[9] I consider whether an integrated pedagogical model of education is adequate for preparing seminarians to recognize and encounter this challenge.

Finally, I use the concept of "authenticity," which the *Ratio* presents as a central component in integral formation for the priesthood, as the lens through which to understand the need for (and the means to achieving) integration.[10] I presuppose the *Ratio*'s position that if seminarians, both individually and as a group, do not sufficiently "demonstrate—and not only in their external behaviour—that they have internalised an authentically priestly way of life. . . . [which] is a sign of a mature choice to give themselves to following Christ in a special way," then this is an obstacle to the efficacy (and continuation) of their formation.[11] In other words, I take seriously the notion that "the holiness of a priest is built upon [human formation] and depends, in large part, upon the authenticity and maturity of his humanity. The lack of a well-structured and balanced personality is

---

9. Congregation for the Clergy, *Ratio* 84. If space were to permit, it would also address the challenges of the experience of one's own weakness, the risk of becoming simply a dispenser of sacred things, and the testing of one's dedication to ministry, which are equally as pertinent and which are integral in the pedagogical model of education in the pastoral programmes in Maynooth from which this chapter draws insight.

10. *Pastores Dabo Vobis* had also recognised this need for future priests to cultivate integrity, "not only out of proper and due growth and realization of self, but also with a view to the ministry," when it stated: "These qualities are needed for them to be balanced people, strong and free, capable of bearing the weight of pastoral responsibilities. They need to be educated to love the truth, to be loyal, to respect every person, to have a sense of justice, to be true to their word, to be genuinely compassionate, to be men of integrity and, especially, to be balanced in judgment and behavior" (PDV 43).

11. Congregation for the Clergy, *Ratio* 131.

a serious and objective hindrance to the continuation of formation for the priesthood."[12]

The Candidate and the Ambient Culture

In his concluding address to the Models of Priestly Formation conference, Archbishop Diarmuid Martin asserted that "[t]he priest in the Ireland of tomorrow must cultivate a faith that is capable of living in a different culture." He suggested that "[m]inistry in the Church in the years to come will . . . be about men and women who have the ability to speak the language of faith authentically in a world where that language may be alien and to speak in a way that attracts." Thus the "different culture" that he envisages is the "secularised society" of a contemporary and future Ireland, "a culture of hostility to Christian values," a "complicated pluralist world," where the language of faith is alien, where it is difficult to identify "the points of contact or insertion for the Christian message," and "where 'secular speak' contains many residual elements of religious thought, but in which the meaning of words has changed." He asked, "How do we prepare seminarians to enter into this culture?"[13]

Similarly, Archbishop Eamon Martin spoke of his own "training" for priesthood, from which he emerged as a newly ordained priest (in the late 1980s) "into a very complex and conflicted world, where we found an increasing disconnect between what our Church stood for, and the prevailing culture around us."[14] From his perspective,

---

12. Congregation for the Clergy, *Ratio* 63.
13. A copy of the "Speaking notes of Most Rev. Diarmuid Martin, Archbishop of Dublin" from the International Symposium *Models of Priestly Formation: Assessing the Past, Reflecting on the Present and Imagining the Future* (18 November 2017) is available at: http://www.dublindiocese.ie/models-of-priestly-formation/.
14. He continued: "I have often wondered, however, could any kind of priestly 'training' (and I use that word 'training' deliberately) have fully prepared me for what lay ahead: the seismic shift that would occur in the early 1990s in Ireland's

the shortcoming of past models of formation was that they "tended to isolate candidates from the world in order to equip them with sufficient spiritual, intellectual and moral strength before they were sent back into the world to engage in the church's mission." Speaking to the present and future models of formation, Diarmuid Martin stressed that though "[s]eminaries must be places where the candidate for ministry can take a step back from [the] business of daily life and begin to discern in prayer and study the deeper Christian values and in such discernment discover himself in a deeper way," this should not be equated with retreating from the world: "there is nothing more dangerous than a seminarian who claims to be leaving the world in a spiritual sense, but who is in fact losing sight of the real world and retreating into a world of his own."[15]

The *Ratio*, for its part, presupposes "the appropriate involvement of the priestly ministry in the culture of today, with all the complex problems that it brings in its wake," and that this "requires openness in priests and that they remain up to date."[16] An appropriate peda-

---

relationship with Church and with priests; the horrendous and shocking child sex abuse scandals; the challenges swept in by a wave of secularisation; the digital revolution and arrival of the internet and social media; the tendency in society towards rampant consumerism, individualism and relativism; the struggle to live a celibate life in a hyper-sexualised culture; the challenge of maintaining good physical and mental health and well-being in an increasingly rushed, stressful and pressurised environment; the decline in vocations to the priesthood and religious life bringing increased demands and a certain loss of morale for those in ministry; enhanced expectations regarding governance and accountability for the temporal goods of the Church?" A copy of the "Opening Address of Archbishop Eamon Martin," at the International Symposium *Models of Priestly Formation: Assessing the Past, Reflecting on the Present and Imagining the Future* (18 November 2017) is available at: https://www.catholicbishops.ie/2017/11/17/opening-address-of-archbishop-eamon-martin-for-international-conference-on-priestly-formation/.

15. Diarmuid Martin, "Speaking notes."
16. Congregation for the Clergy, *Ratio* 84.

gogical model for the preparation of future priests should thereby cultivate an openness in the seminarian to culture so that, while he discovers himself in discernment, he does not become cut off from the real world. Rather, his formation should enable him to remain up to date with that world or culture.

This is one of the grounding principles of the pastoral formation programmes at Maynooth.[17] They aim to create a basic supervised and supported structure for study that enables candidates to experience the "real world," most often through the experience of living and working in a parish.[18] The parish is given particular importance as a

---

17. At Maynooth, the Pontifical University provides the course of studies undertaken by seminarians of St. Patrick's College as part of their formation for ordained priesthood. A significant stage of this course of studies is a phase of intense pastoral formation where the candidates undertake either a diploma or higher diploma in pastoral theology. These programmes are commonly referred to as "the pastoral year." In contrast to the "pastoral stage" as outlined in the *Ratio* (which is intended to take place in the period between the end of formation in the seminary and priestly ordination), this phase of formation takes place midway through the stage of theological studies. This is consistent with the understanding in *Pastores Dabo Vobis* that pastoral theology "needs to be studied . . . as the true and genuine theological discipline that it is," as a "scientific reflection on the Church as she is built up daily, by the power of the Spirit, in history," involving the candidate "in certain pastoral services" or "pastoral 'experiences' . . . which can last a considerable amount of time" and that are "always in harmony with their other educational commitments"; it is "a type of formation meant not only to ensure scientific, pastoral competence and practical skill, but also and especially a way of being in communion with the very sentiments and behavior of Christ the good shepherd" (57). The Pastoral programmes are thus well placed within the stage of theological studies, and candidates have reported that completing a year of pastoral formation (where ministry practice is integrated with theological study and reflection) has better enabled them to enter into a deeper understanding of their theological studies on returning to their baccalaureate in divinity programme.

18. The Pontifical University has a long history of collaborating with "teaching parishes" across the island of Ireland in the preparation of candidates for

context for pastoral experience, because it is understood as a "living cell of local and specialized pastoral work in which [candidates] will find themselves faced with the kind of problems they will meet in their future ministry."[19] In accordance with *Pastores Dabo Vobis*, the programmes aspire to give candidates "an initial and gradual experience of ministry" so that "future priests will be able to be inserted into the living pastoral tradition of their particular church. They will learn to open the horizon of their mind and heart to the missionary dimension of the Church's life."[20]

This gradual and immersive experience in the real life and ministry of the church inevitably enables an encounter with the culture of today. This does not mean, however, that this encounter is something new (though with guidance and supervision it might be perceived as if for the first time or in a new way). This is because it is not possible for students to retreat from and to stand outside of culture, and return to it in ministry to meet it for the first time; they are always already involved in culture. In fact, students "do not so much see and believe [their] own society's patterns, thoughts, and feelings; rather [they] approach life through them."[21]

---

ministry. For many years, parishes have given our students great welcome and have been generous in providing a wealth of learning opportunities in diverse ministry settings, sharing their collective wisdom and effective approaches to ministry, and showing our students the reality of life and activity in our church today. Teaching parish representatives, known as "placement contact persons," have facilitated our students' ongoing learning in real situations, and provided on-site mentoring on their experiences, which greatly complements the learning that takes place in the classroom setting in Maynooth.

19. John Paul II, *Pastores Dabo Vobis* 58.
20. John Paul II, *Pastores Dabo Vobis*, 58.
21. Michael A. Conway, "Ministry in Transition," *The Furrow* 65, no. 3 (March 2014): 132. Subsequent paragraphs are indebted to the reflections of Michael A. Conway, Professor of Faith and Culture at Maynooth, and priest of the Diocese of Galway, who has spoken and written about the changes in Irish

Thus the culture that might be perceived by one generation of the presbyterate as "different" (from the culture in which they were raised and/or initially practiced ministry) is quite familiar to current and future generations of seminarians since they grow/mature within it, or are native to it. In other words, the seismic changes that are perceived by one as different from his culture (or time) of origin are embedded deep in the fabric of the other's (cultural) identity. The *Ratio* itself acknowledged that those who begin the seminary journey are "already naturally quite adept and immersed in" the world and its instruments.[22] Thus even in those stages of seminary life, when candidates step back from the business (or busyness) of daily life to discern in prayer and study, in a certain sense their culture remains with them, shaping their understanding of reality, of God, their expressions of faith, and thereby influencing their process of discernment and engagement with formation.

In a focused and structured way, the Pontifical University's pastoral programmes aspire to provide an opportunity for each candidate to remain attentive to, and up-to-date with, the culture of which his is already a part.[23] Indeed, it is a presupposition of these programmes that through the daily encounter with people and diverse situations in ministry, and through reflective practice and theological reflection on those encounters and experiences, the candidate discovers himself in a deeper way: he seeks to understand how cultural and historical

---

culture and the impact these have on priestly ministry today. Here some of his insights are included in order to consider how they might be relevant to seminary life and the journey of formation towards priesthood in particular.

22. The *Ratio* was referring in this instance to the digital world in particular; however, the same holds true for the world or culture in general.

23. If there are some seminarians who have left their own countries to receive formation for the priesthood in Ireland, engaging with the challenge of cultural differences becomes paramount. The candidate is enabled to become aware of his culture of origin as well as the distinctiveness of the Irish/Western European cultural context. The richness of each culture must be adequately respected.

conditioning may influence his thoughts, presumptions, values, practices, etc., as well as the beliefs and actions of others he may encounter in life and ministry. Through the ministry experiences in teaching parishes and academic studies at Maynooth, students learn to look to the ambient world and culture to understand their own faith and the present faith experiences of others, while simultaneously looking to the inherited faith experiences in Scripture and tradition.[24]

This approach is essential for opening candidates' minds and hearts to the missionary dimension of the church's life. Preparing future priests to engage with culture is not about training them in a public relations exercise in learning how to make the church more attractive to a culture that is other or alien: "That neither respects the integrity of the mission of the church as a life that renews itself, nor takes seriously the very culture within which it seeks to enable gospel life."[25] Rather, preparing the candidate to participate in the one mission entrusted by Christ to his church means learning to recognize that:

> To be Church is to be Church in a culture; to proclaim the good news is to proclaim the good news in a culture. And when the culture changes, so too must the Church (if it is to be faithful to itself) . . . the Church is not outside of, or over against the culture; it is, rather, within it; and this has a huge bearing on its future form and future activity (pastoral or otherwise).[26]

Therefore, "Seminaries should form missionary disciples who are 'in love' with the Master, shepherds 'with the smell of sheep,' *who live in their midst* to bring the mercy of God to them."[27] If future priests do

---

24. Stephen B. Bevans, *Models of Contextual Theology*, rev. and expanded ed. (Maryknoll, NY: Orbis Books, 2002), 5; See also Michael A. Conway, "Changing Foundations: Identity, Church and Culture," *The Furrow* 69, no. 2 (February 2018): 91.

25. Conway, "Ministry in Transition," 143.

26. Conway, "Changing Foundations," 91.

27. Congregation for the Clergy, *Ratio*, intro., sec. 3, par. 7 (emphasis added).

not live and work in the community of the church as men "of [their] own culture and [their] own times," it will be very difficult for them "to discern God at work in . . . culture," or "to preach the gospel in an idiom that will be heard by those whom [they] encounter"; and it would be extremely difficult for others to experience them "as people of good news and gospel action."[28]

The Cultural Ethic of Authenticity

One feature of the ambient culture that likely (and perhaps unavoidably) shapes the identity of those beginning their seminary journey today is the value of "authenticity," which has moved to center stage in our culture.[29] It has become crystallized around the idea that each one of us has his/her own way of realizing our humanity, and this is how one ought to live. Thus the search for one's "true self" becomes essential, creating one's own identity according to what one finds most meaningful. This means each person constructs his/her own identity against a background that is in movement: "I am in the process of identifying who I am for myself and for others."[30] This dynamic might be helpfully described using the language of pilgrimage:

> The pilgrim is that figure that makes his or her own way, alone, even if part of a group, on a path that he or she chooses in order to seek and discover something personal, something that can be named as authentic, and something that will help in establishing meaning in life. It is a journey with stages; to a greater degree you choose the path; you may skip some stages that are not for you; you may abandon the path for a while; you may take it up at a later stage; or you may go down a different path.[31]

---

28. Conway, "Ministry in Transition," 144.
29. Conway, "Ministry in Transition," 134.
30. Michael A. Conway, "Transmission of Faith," *The Furrow* 69, no. 5 (May 2018): 261–62.
31. Conway, "Transmission of Faith," 262.

In this context, ordained priesthood may be seen and understood to be a personal calling, what the seminarian desires to do with his life (albeit on the basis of a personally discerned vocation from God), what is authentic for him.[32] Priesthood may be thus experienced as one choice among many, and because of the mobility that comes with having multiple options, joining the seminary is simply not a once-and-for-all decision; he can move off again if it is not right for him (at this time), and/or take it up at a later stage; or if this place is not right for him, choose to go elsewhere. This makes it difficult to maintain a seminary community over time, or to have an approach to formation that meets the needs of a spectrum of people. Increasingly, individuals "expect a specific and tailored response to their presence in the community."[33] This raises important questions about the sustainability, consistency, and quality of the formation journey or process.

The significant cultural "good" of discovering one's own personal path (or calling) that is authentic, coupled with a more critical spirit in Irish society and a less deferential attitude toward all authority, means that authenticity is contrasted with conformity (i.e., to surrendering to a way of life that is imposed from the outside, whether by religion, or previous generations of family, or political establishment, etc.). Individuals realize that "there is no neutral transaction or communication. There are agendas at play, there is politics at work, and there is almost always self-interest in the detail."[34] The authority

---

32. Conway, "Ministry in Transition," 146. This tendency ignores, of course, the ecclesial dimension of vocation—that the community is itself an agent of God's call: "[T]here is also a certain tendency to view the bond between human beings and God in an individualistic and self-centered way, as if God's call reached the individual by a direct route without in any way passing through the community. . . . [This] makes it impossible to recognize and accept joyfully the ecclesial dimension which naturally marks every Christian vocation, and the priestly vocation in particular" (*Pastores Dabo Vobis* 37).

33. Conway, "Ministry in Transition," 137.

34. Conway, "Ministry in Transition," 139.

of a person's position is no longer sufficient for justifying belief or compliance with what he or she communicates or requires. What this means for the life of the present-day seminarian is that he will likely have developed a critical distance from those within the community of formators. The course of studies or formative programme that they present will not be simply believed and accepted: each will be assessed according to whether the candidate perceives them to be "true" or "authentic" in preparation for his path to priesthood.

If what is presented is mostly (or entirely) at odds with the candidate's own understanding, this might become manifest in some form of resistance to the studies or formation programme; or the candidate might respond with indignation, if those in positions of authority do not act according to the candidate's expectations of what is required of them because of their positions. Two such dynamics or experiences have had an impact on seminary life at Maynooth in recent times, both undoubtedly harmful, and not just for the seminary community but also for the integrity of the seminarians' journey towards priesthood. The first is voicing discontent/disapproval about seminary life and culture in the public sphere, but doing so anonymously and thus without accountability; and the second is responding with an approach of "keeping your head down," having an appearance of meeting external demands, biding time until ordination.[35] Both are contrary to the caution of the *Ratio* that the priest "cannot limit himself simply to demonstrating a 'veneer of virtuous habits,' a merely

---

35. Ironically, the latter response is ultimately counterproductive to the drive for authenticity. However, perhaps it is indirectly caused or perpetuated by an underdeveloped understanding of obedience directed to those with authority within seminary communities. The form of obedience, which the *Ratio* asserts is the duty of formators to inculcate in students, is one which should respect interior freedom: "[I]t is the duty of formators, therefore, to train seminarians in a true and mature obedience, by exercising authority with prudence, and encouraging them to give their assent, also their *interior assent*, in a peaceful and *sincere* manner" (*Ratio* 109; emphasis added).

external and formalistic obedience to abstract principles. Rather, he is called to act with great interior freedom."[36] Whatever the individual seminarian's response, it is important to remember that what might appear to those in authority as a rebuttal or rejection may simply be from the candidate's perspective "a responsible reservation in the face of an important life choice."[37]

One further dimension of this cultural drive for authenticity is that a visible number of young adults, including a number of candidates discerning for the priesthood, are choosing to follow the path of (what would appear to be) a very traditional form of faith. One of their core beliefs is that "being faithful to the gospel and the reality of a living church means being concerned primarily with preserving what has been inherited from the past: taking the 'tradition' in all its complexity and handing it on to a new generation or group as perfectly intact as possible."[38] They look to the past to reappropriate the language, customs, dress, and practices of what they perceive to be a traditional identity, to shape and structure their own identity in the present. Cultural commentators see in this dynamic a phenomenon that is "reactionary":

> [I]t is reacting to the secularising tendencies in the culture. It asserts a form of public religiosity in the face of a culture that is judged no longer to give room to religion, or, perhaps better, to a particular expression of religion. . . . It is a phenomenon that has emerged in a specific cultural context: namely, liberal Western democracy. In terms of the Catholic Church in Ireland the phenomenon has emerged in about the last fifteen years or so and is reactionary not just from within the wider culture, but also from within the Church itself, where it is presented as saving the reality of religion from what are perceived to be destructive developments in the post-Council era.[39]

---

36. Congregation for the Clergy, *Ratio* 41.
37. Conway, "Ministry in Transition," 140.
38. Conway, "Ministry in Transition," 141.
39. Conway, "Transmission of Faith," 265.

Since this outlook is reactionary, proponents might view themselves as being authentically and justifiably countercultural. Paradoxically, like their peers in broader society, they are following the demands of their culture, and seeking to define their own identities. The risk when this concerns someone preparing for the priesthood is that, by adopting this position prior to or at an early stage of formation, there might be very little real engagement with the complexity of the Christian tradition or with the history of the church's journey in and through time.[40] This poses a challenge for educators and formators in a seminary community, who endeavor to achieve an integrated formation programme, and so genuinely shape the identity of the seminarian and future priest. Of course, since authenticity is actually a central component in integral formation for the priesthood, it is of great concern if this dynamic actually creates a pseudo or false self, leading to what formation is meant to avoid: namely, fragmentation, polarisation, excesses, superficiality or partiality.

Integrity and the Virtue of Authenticity

Pastoral formation programmes, like those at Maynooth, have the formidable task of employing pedagogical practices that will find the proper balance between the different dimensions of formation—intellectual, pastoral, spiritual, and human. Though the holiness of a priest is built upon human formation in particular, and depends, in large part, upon the authenticity and maturity of the candidate's humanity, educators have to ask themselves honestly: to what degree do they influence or shape the developing character of candidates for the priesthood in a way that aids in their journey of growth towards authentic maturity? Richard Gula observes

> [T]he kinds of habits we form prior to entering ministry influence, more than we might want to admit, the kind of minister we will

---

40. Conway, "Transmission of Faith," 265.

become and the style our ministry will take. It is not unusual to see the character a candidate brings through the front door of a formation program to be, by and large, the very character that walks out the back door at the end of the process. Some fine-tuning may go on, but radical changes are rare. People generally stay "in character." We generally dismiss atypical behavior or give it little attention because, since it is so uncharacteristic of the candidate, we feel that it does not represent their true self.[41]

The task of forming a candidate's character thus begins long before he enters formal preparation for priesthood. Often it is the candidate's preexisting beliefs or espoused values and embedded practices that create challenges in the process of formation. Foster et al. discovered that "students may resist or subvert those faculty intentions for their spiritual and professional formation" because these are perceived as contrary to their existing beliefs which are "deeply rooted in family traditions and local or regional subcultures," or where they have "internalized (and in some cases appropriated) prevailing views of race, gender, social and economic class, and religious diversity."[42]

Despite the difficult task of integrating human formation within pastoral programmes, it remains a worthwhile task, because it "emphasizes the connection between what ministry needs to do to promote the reign of God and the personal strengths we need to pursue it."[43] To acknowledge that personal strengths are needed to pursue this goal is to recognize that ministering ethically is not only a matter of doing one's duty or following a rule: the virtuous minister does not "go through the motions" because he or she is obligated to do so, because he or she is being supervised or is accountable to someone in author-

---

41. Richard M. Gula, SS, *Just Ministry: Professional Ethics for Pastoral Ministers* (New York: Paulist Press, 2010), 75.

42. Charles R. Foster, Lisa Dahill, Larry Golemon, Barbara Wang Tolentino, *Educating Clergy: Teaching Practices and the Pastoral Imagination* (San Francisco, CA: Jossey-Bass, 2006), 102.

43. Gula, *Just Ministry*, 46.

ity, or indeed to avoid scandal; rather, the pastoral minister strives for excellence, to ensure that ministry is "a true expression of one's self," and that all ministerial activity corresponds with an "internally, self-directing commitment to what promotes human flourishing."[44] In other words, he or she strives to be a minister of integrity.

The virtue of integrity is among the list of those virtues which the *Ratio* suggests "it is important to inculcate . . . in those called to priesthood and pastoral ministry."[45] It would be understandable to simply think of such integrity as requiring consistency between the candidate's espoused beliefs and his everyday practice, or even consistency with the norms and traditions of the Christian faith that he is expected to uphold. However, genuine integrity requires much more: "The pastor will learn to leave behind preconceived certainties and will not think of his ministry as a series of things to be done or norms to be applied, but will make his life a 'place' for listening openly to God and to his brothers and sisters."[46] Integrity therefore concerns the person's whole life, which is placed in an attitude of openness and receptivity to others and to God. It is only possible to appreciate how one can attain such a life of integrity by considering the person's journey of human maturity, which has as its goal "the authentic realization of the self."[47]

The concept of "authenticity" would not prove useful in this context, however, if the search for the authentic self could only be achieved at the expense of, or without recourse to, the other.[48] Therefore, the risk of posing authenticity as a central component in the formation process

---

44. Gula, *Just Ministry*, 67.
45. Congregation for the Clergy, *Ratio* 115.
46. Congregation for the Clergy, *Ratio* 120.
47. John Paul II, *Pastores Dabo Vobis* 44.
48. "The first source of worry is individualism. . . . We live in a world where people have a right to choose for themselves their own pattern of life, to decide in conscience what convictions to espouse, to determine the shape of their lives in a whole host of ways that their ancestors couldn't control." Charles Taylor, *The Ethics of Authenticity* (London: Harvard University Press, 1991), 2.

is that it is susceptible to the critique of subjectivism or moral relativism: it can be said to involve "a centering on the self and a concomitant shutting out, or even unawareness, of the greater issues or concerns that transcend the self"; accordingly, people would be "called upon to be true to themselves and to seek their own self-fulfillment," and even to determine for themselves what this self-fulfillment consists of.[49] This outlook makes self-fulfillment the major value in life and recognizes few (if any) external moral demands or serious commitments to others.[50] However, Charles Taylor argues that ignoring whatever transcends the self and seeking individual self-fulfillment are deviant forms of the "moral ideal" of authenticity.[51]

Properly understood, Taylor advocates that the ideal of authenticity calls for a recognition of the relational or "dialogical" feature of human life, whereby we become capable of understanding ourselves and defining our personal identities, through the rich modes of expression we acquire in our exchanges with others: he suggests that we define our identities "always in dialogue with, sometimes in struggle against, the identities our significant others want to recognize in us."[52]

> My discovering my identity doesn't mean that I work it out in isolation but that I negotiate it through dialogue, partly overt, partly internalized, with others. That is why the development of an ideal of inwardly generated identity gives a new and crucial importance to recognition. My own identity crucially depends on my dialogical relations with others.[53]

In addition, the ideal of authenticity involves recognizing the "preexisting horizons of significance," or the larger social and cosmic

---

49. Taylor, *The Ethics of Authenticity*, 4, 14.
50. Taylor, 55.
51. Taylor, 15, 22.
52. Taylor, 32–33.
53. Taylor, 47.

order, of which we are a part and which lay claim on us; in these horizons, "some things are worthwhile and others less so, and still others not at all," but we cannot ignore the demands they place on us.[54] These are the demands that emanate from beyond ourselves.[55]

For Walter E. Conn, too, there is no self outside of relationship.[56] He theorises that "the fundamental desire of the self is to transcend itself in relationship—to the world, to others, and to God."[57] This is the "radical desire" of "every person . . . to reach out, to move beyond, to transcend the self."[58] Conn argues that the drive for self-transcendence is a "criterion of personal authenticity" and it stands in "complete opposition to both self-sacrifice and self-fulfilment, as these are commonly understood."[59] In this understanding, if self-sacrifice means "a denial, renunciation, abnegation, or any other negation of the true self," and if self-fulfillment focuses on satisfying our own "ego-centric self-interests," in fulfilling "our every want and wish," there is little self-transcendence.[60]

In contrast to these deviant forms, Conn asserts that "self-transcendence supports the gospel's paradoxical view that authentic self-realization results not from a self-centred effort to fulfil one's every wish, but from a movement beyond oneself in an attempt to

---

54. Taylor, 38.

55. "Only if I exist in a world in which history, or the demands of nature, or the needs of my fellow human beings, or the duties of citizenship, or the call of God, or something else of this order *matters* crucially, can I define an identity for myself that is not trivial. Authenticity is not the enemy of demands that emanate from beyond the self; it supposes such demands" (Taylor, 40–41).

56. Walter E. Conn, "Self-Transcendence, the True Self, and Self-Love," *Pastoral Psychology* 46, no. 5 (1998): 326.

57. Walter E. Conn, "Understanding the Self in Self-Transcendence," *Pastoral Psychology* 46, no. 1 (1997): 3.

58. Conn, "Self-Transcendence, the True Self, and Self-Love," 323.

59. Conn, 324.

60. Conn, 324, 331.

realize the good of others."[61] The sense of self-sacrifice that is compatible with this understanding of self-transcendence can require one to "empty" oneself, "to give up everything else, even life itself, in loving service of the neighbor."[62] This self-emptying is an act of loving others. Conn maintains that "we love ourselves in an authentic way by loving others": "Loving others *is* loving ourselves because acting for the true good of others (their growth, happiness) is acting for our own good (realization of our capacity for self-transcendence)."[63] In this way, self-emptying does not constitute a negation of the self; rather it is a realisation of one's true authentic self.

The concept of authenticity, rightly understood, leads one on a journey towards "a mature and responsible freedom" that

> expresses itself in convinced and heartfelt obedience to the "truth of one's own being, to the "meaning" of one's own existence, that is to the "sincere gift of self" as the way and fundamental content of the authentic realization of self. Thus understood, freedom requires the person to be truly master of oneself, determined to fight and overcome the different forms of selfishness and individualism which threaten the life of each one, ready to open out to others, generous in dedication and service to one's neighbor.[64]

---

61. Conn, 324.

62. Walter E. Conn, *Christian Conversion: A Developmental Interpretation of Autonomy and Surrender* (Eugene, OR: Wipf & Stock, 1986), 23.

63. Conn, "Self-Transcendence, the True Self, and Self-Love," 331.

64. John Paul II, *Pastores Dabo Vobis* 44. It seems pertinent to acknowledge, at this point, the lifelong or ongoing character of the journey of formation: true mastery of oneself is elusive, conditioned as one is by cultural context. One can never fully understand the cultural matrix of which one is a part, though one might diligently strive to do so. Similarly, it is a lifelong task to strive for self-transcendence avoiding the poles of self-sacrifice on the one hand or self-fulfillment on the other. The central point here is that we define our identities in dialogue with others (in relationship or community), and that within this context a *sincere* gift of self is indispensable for the realisation of authentic self.

The true authentic self, therefore, can only be found through the sincere gift of self.[65] Selfishness, understood as seeking the fulfillment of one's own egocentric wants and desires, threatens the realisation of the self one is meant to be. Moreover, since this drive for the authenticity of self-transcendence is the "divine life within the human person," its realisation "culminates in a personal relationship with God."[66] To discover one's true self is to discover God.[67] Thus, a greater understanding of the self, and one's relationality, will help the minister "relate more authentically with God and others."[68]

Conclusion

The determination to adopt an integrated pedagogical model of formation is grounded in the notion that it is the whole person, with all that he is and all that he possesses, who will be at the Lord's service in the Christian community. A candidate cannot make a complete gift of himself, which ordained priesthood requires, without striving to understand or realize his authentic self.[69] Since authenticity

---

65. Second Vatican Council, Pastoral Constitution on the Church in the Modern World (*Gaudium et Spes*) 24.

66. Conn, "Self-Transcendence, the True Self, and Self-Love," 324.

67. Thomas Merton, *New Seeds of Contemplation* (New York: New Directions, 1972), 36.

68. United States Conference of Catholic Bishops, *Co-Workers in the Vineyard of the Lord: A Resource for Guiding the Development of Lay Ecclesial Ministry* (Washington, DC: USCCB, December 2005), 36.

69. Kathleen A. Cahalan describes integration as an auspicious goal for theological educators: "We know the fully integrated student-minister, the person with full knowledge, complete competence in all ministerial skills, and a fully mature vocational identity is beyond our reach; it is only anticipated in seminary but discovered and refined in the practice of ministry." And yet formation programmes must "attend intentionally" to how the various capacities and facets of the seminarian and his life "are merging into a whole" (Kathleen A. Cahalan,

cannot be achieved without dialogical relations with others, educators should strive to incorporate interpersonal engagement between faculty and candidates, and peer group sessions to provide meaningful moments of exchange and growth."[70] Moreover, supervised ministry experiences in parish contexts should enable the candidate to move beyond himself and realize the good of others. Ideally, the importance of integration would be recognized across the stages of formation and not be reserved to dedicated pastoral formation programmes.

"Introducing Ministry and Fostering Integration," *For Life Abundant: Practical Theology, Theological Education, and Christian Ministry* [Cambridge, UK: Eerdmans, 2008], 113).

70. In the pastoral programmes at Maynooth, monthly one-to-one consultation sessions with staff mentors, frequent mentoring sessions with on-site placement contact people, and weekly peer supervision and theological reflection groups are a few of the methods used to encourage such moments of encounter and exchange.

Chapter Eight

An International Perspective on Priestly Formation

Ronald D. Witherup, PSS

Introduction

One of the great privileges of being superior general of an international group of diocesan priests dedicated to initial and ongoing formation of priests (and formators) has been the ability to travel widely and experience "on the ground" the reality of priestly formation on five continents. The Society of St. Sulpice is currently present in seventeen countries on these five continents, and I have benefitted enormously from the opportunity to assess the quality of priestly formation in some twenty Sulpician institutions of priestly formation around the world, and to have visited others. My task in this chapter is to identify and explain from my experience an international perspective on priestly formation and to suggest challenges that might be anticipated as the future unfolds.

I proceed in three stages. The first will summarize from a historical and experiential point of view the various models of priestly formation for diocesan priests that are in current use throughout the world. Second, I propose some evaluative comments on priestly formation that arise from this international perspective. Finally, I outline some major challenges in priestly formation that I envision on the basis of the expectations announced in the revised *Ratio Fundamentalis Institutionis Sacerdotalis* and the realities faced by a multiplicity of international contexts.[1]

I. Models of Priestly Formation

Since at least the time of the American theologian Cardinal Avery Dulles (1918-2008),[2] theologians have used the concept of "models" as a convenient heuristic tool in theological discussions. Regarding contemporary seminary formation, one author has proposed five main models: Trent (the Roman model), the Sulpicians (the French model), *Pastores Dabo Vobis*, the Neocatechumenal Way (based on the spirituality of the founder, Kiko Arguello), and the Paris model (based upon the vision of Cardinal Jean-Marie Lustiger).[3] While three of these seem to me to describe true institutional *models* (Trent, Sulpicians, Paris)—as I will describe below—the remaining two (*Pastores Dabo Vobis* and the Neocatechumenal Way) constitute "spiritualities" of priestly formation rather than models. Thus, *Pastores Dabo Vobis* provides an overarching vision of priestly formation that marks *all*

---

1. Congregation for the Clergy, *The Gift of the Priestly Vocation: Ratio Fundamentalis Institutionis Sacerdotalis* (London: CTS Publications, 2017). The *Ratio* itself is heavily reliant upon the groundbreaking post-synodal apostolic exhortation of Pope St. John Paul II, *Pastores Dabo Vobis* (25 March 1992), whose "four-pillar" model has strongly marked not only priestly formation but formation of deacons, catechists, and other ministers in the church. The *Ratio* now uses the word "dimension" rather than "pillar," likely to lend a less rigid image in formation.

2. See Avery Dulles, *Models of the Church* (Garden City, NY: Doubleday, 1974). Later editions (1987 and 2002) expanded the original models, and in 1983 the same author applied the notion of "models" to divine revelation itself.

3. See Charles M. Murphy, *Models of Priestly Formation: Past, Present, and Future* (New York: Crossroad, 2006).

post-Vatican II seminary formation, especially after the promulgation of the revised *Ratio*. And the Neocatechumenal Way's approach to priestly formation is based on a distinct spirituality of the movement's lay founder. Both of these are less structural models than variations of priestly formation based upon distinct spiritual outlooks.

The revised *Ratio* itself acknowledges at the beginning of its last chapter, on "criteria and norms" (RF 188), that different forms of seminary formation exist, but they are not enunciated in detail. What is clear, as the document states explicitly, is that a seminary is "more than a building"; it is a "community of formation." In my experience around the world, I believe we can point to four primary models of seminary formation for diocesan priesthood, with allowance for some differences of design or function in accord with certain cultural preferences or spiritual underpinnings.[4]

A. Freestanding Seminaries

The first model, and the one that seems to be the presumed ideal in the *Ratio*, is the freestanding seminary. This may be either diocesan (sponsored by one diocese or other entity to serve priestly formation in a geographic region) or interdiocesan (sponsored by a number of different dioceses, perhaps in conjunction with other entities or in a geographical region, in order to conserve resources). Such freestanding seminaries are often owned and operated by one proprietor. For instance, there are seminaries owned and operated by individual dioceses, by Benedictine monasteries, by the Sulpicians, or by an incorporated board of diocesan priests, but they are usually at the service of multiple dioceses. In many cases, there are various practical considerations for establishing interdiocesan or regional freestanding

---

4. The most thorough current sociological analysis of contemporary seminary formation is Katarina Schuth, *Seminary Formation: Recent History—Current Circumstances—New Directions* (Collegeville, MN: Liturgical Press, 2016), but it addresses exclusively the North American context.

seminaries. These include the desire to share the financial burdens of maintaining such institutions, to ensure adequate numbers of seminarians, and also to minimize the number of trained formation personnel—often in short supply—needed to ensure good formation. What distinguishes all of these freestanding models is that every aspect of formation is addressed, we might say, "under one roof." That is, all four dimensions of priestly formation—human, spiritual, intellectual, and pastoral—are conducted "in-house" and are under the direct supervision of the seminary formation team.[5] So, the daily regimen of prayer and worship, the instruction in the classroom, the individual and communal sessions for human and pastoral formation, and community life activities all take place within the context of the seminary community. Naturally, most seminaries of this type need to use the services of external or adjunct formators, especially in teaching courses and in supervising outside pastoral placements, or perhaps even in offering spiritual direction. I know of no instance where a formation team in a freestanding seminary provides all aspects of formation without any outside assistance.

Under this general category of seminary, another important distinction is pertinent. Since the seventeenth century, there have been primarily two subtypes of freestanding seminaries: the Roman model and the Sulpician model. Each of these has certain defining aspects.

The Roman model is rooted in the vision of St. Charles Borromeo, the reforming bishop of Milan,[6] who responded to the call of the

---

5. This means that a formation team member likely supervises even the pastoral placement, which is actually performed outside the seminary, whether in a parish, a hospital, a prison, a nursing home, or a soup kitchen, etc.

6. While Borromeo was not actually the first bishop to found a seminary after Trent, his was the first *major* effort to implement the council's vision; it became a point of reference for later attempts to improve priestly formation. See John Tracy Ellis, "A Short History of Seminary Education: II—Trent to Today," in *Seminary Education in a Time of Change*, James Michael Lee and Louis J. Putz, eds. (St. Louis: Fides, 1965), 30–81.

Council of Trent (1545–1563) by establishing several seminaries in his large, wealthy diocese to ensure good quality formation of priests.[7] Other Italian bishops followed his example and founded seminaries. Borromeo was thus a model reforming bishop whose authoritative vision helped to renew the church in his day. Some decades later, in France, other visionaries were responding to the same expressed need in their particular historical context. I refer to certain holy priests, mostly members of the so-called French school of spirituality, like Vincent de Paul, Jean Eudes, and especially the Sulpician founder Jean-Jacques Olier, who established highly successful seminaries for the training of priests precisely so that they could contribute to the greater reform of the church. Olier, for instance, explicitly states: "God wishes to use me to renew his Church by instructing many priests in the ecclesiastical spirit so that they will then go forth to serve God wherever He is pleased to call them."[8] Olier believed that if one could renew the clergy, the whole church could be renewed.

These models developed over time, and we can briefly outline the current differences in the two approaches. The Roman model is, by design, hierarchical. Thus, the superior (rector) is truly the governing agent of the seminary. He convokes the formation team, makes the decisions, and usually writes the seminarians' evaluations and communicates with the bishops and vocation directors. In the Roman model, there is only one spiritual director for the house, and he gives the spiritual conferences, organizes the spiritual life program, and is available to all the seminarians for consultation and the sacrament

---

7. A concise summary of the early history of seminaries is given in Joseph M. White, *The Diocesan Seminary in the United States: A History from the 1780s to the Present* (Notre Dame, IN: University of Notre Dame Press, 1989), 1–23, and John Tracy Ellis, "A Short History of Seminary Education: I—The Apostolic Age to Trent," in Lee and Putz, *Seminary Education*, 1–29.

8. Jean-Jacques Olier, Mémoires autographes, 3, 85 (my trans.), *La Compagnie des Prêtres de Saint-Sulpice, Service des Archives*, Paris, France.

of reconciliation. Although some formators may teach classes in this model, more often the seminarians take courses outside the seminary, taught by external experts who do not participate formally in formation discussions.

The Sulpician model, as already envisioned by Father Olier who began his seminary in conjunction with his parish, St. Sulpice (whence the name "Sulpicians"), of which he was pastor and which today is found in the sixth arrondissement in the heart of Paris, was collegial. The superior (rector) is viewed as the animator or facilitator of a team of formators. He does not make policy decisions on his own but brings to the formation team recommendations to consider. Like the other formators, the superior votes on such policy matters, although he has a certain moral authority and the capacity to break a tie vote. In addition, Sulpician seminaries do not have only one main spiritual director.[9] Every priest on the formation team makes himself available to be freely chosen by a number of seminarians for whom he will serve as a spiritual director, entirely in the internal forum. In addition, each formator serves as a formation advisor or mentor in the external forum for a number of seminarians, for whom he is responsible for writing the final evaluation and sharing with the formation team pertinent observations about the seminarian's readiness to move on to the next step. In Sulpician houses that are freestanding seminaries, almost all the members of the formation team also teach academic courses in their field of expertise, and at least one person is charged with overseeing pastoral assignments. What is essential in this model is the equal participation of all the members of the formation team at virtually every level of formation. In addition, unlike the Roman model, the formators live with the seminarians and share their common life:

---

9. In recent years, many Sulpician houses nonetheless have adopted a modified Roman practice by naming a spiritual director for the house, but the post is strictly for purpose of organizing the details of the spiritual life program (e.g., days of recollection, outside confessors, and annual retreats).

prayer, worship, meals, and even common recreation (within certain parameters that protect professional boundaries).

The freestanding seminary remains the most common model around the world. While there are clearly variations and adaptations, most run either according to the Roman model or the Sulpician model, regardless of whether they are diocesan, inter-diocesan, or regional. In recent years, there has been some crossover of aspects of these two systems. For instance, some Roman model seminaries have adopted a common practice characteristic of Sulpician seminaries in which each seminarian works with a formation advisor (mentor) in the external forum. And many Sulpician seminaries have a designated "spiritual director" to coordinate the spiritual life program (see *Ratio* 136). One of the possible disadvantages of the freestanding model is the lack of connection to the real pastoral world. Sometimes the transition from seminary to parish is difficult, in part because the seminary is almost like a "womb" where everything is provided, including a secure structure, a regimen of prayer, and built-in community.

B. University Model

The second type of seminary is also well known, namely, the university model. In such instances the seminary is essentially a "house of formation," a residence where seminarians are formed by community life and by multiple aspects of human and spiritual formation. The intellectual dimension, however, is fulfilled by attending outside classes, often taught at pontifical universities or institutes. Numerous seminaries follow this model,[10] and it is the one adopted by many religious communities who have ties to consortiums or collectivities

---

10. In the Sulpician system, for example, there are Theological College in Washington, DC, in association with The Catholic University of America, Saint Joseph's Seminary in Edmonton, Alberta, Canada, in association with Newman College, and (as of mid-2018) Assumption Seminary in San Antonio, Texas, in association with the Oblate School of Theology. A similar model is the Séminaire

of higher education[11] to provide intellectual formation, while the religious houses themselves provide the rest of priestly formation.

A potential disadvantage of this model is the possible separation of the intellectual dimension from the other three. If accommodation is not made to ensure that the professors teaching the courses see their input also as formative—with the ability to inform seminary formators of possible problems of comportment of seminarians or irresponsibility—then the academic component is simply seen as a way to *educate* seminarians, but not necessarily to *form* them.

C. Parish-Based Model

We Sulpicians know well that our own seminary model began in the context of Father Olier's parish. Olier believed diocesan priests should be formed by diocesan priests.[12] In fact, Olier used the parish as a kind of "laboratory" for the formation of future priests, ensuring that throughout their years of formation they would have concrete experiences in a pastoral setting that would allow them immediately to apply their spiritual and intellectual formation in pastoral situations. As time went on, however, the Holy See became insistent on priestly formation being conducted apart in a seminary setting, sometimes almost monastic in conception. Even the model of spiritual life for diocesan priests is clearly based upon the monastic model of prayer in community, and it obviously is foundational in all seminaries.

---

des Carmes in Paris, in association with Institut Catholique de Paris, and there are numerous similar arrangements in Rome.

11. For example, Catholic Theological Union in Chicago, Illinois, serves a number of religious communities who maintain separate houses of formation; the Union assures the academic classes and degree programs. Likewise, the Graduate Theological Union in Berkeley, California, offers a similar setup but in an ecumenical context; various Protestant seminaries are also involved.

12. To this day, Sulpicians remain diocesan priests, a society of apostolic life of pontifical right (*C.I.C.* 731.1), who must obtain their bishop's permission to enter the Society. A transfer of canonical jurisdiction takes place when the priest joins the Society, normally for life.

In 1984, however, in an attempt to meet the needs of a changing world, Cardinal Jean-Marie Lustiger (1926–2007), archbishop of Paris, founded what has become known as the "Paris model" of seminary formation, which is essentially parish based. Currently, there are nine formation houses in the Paris program, each located in a parish and supervised by a local superior (usually the pastor) and his adjunct.[13] Like the university model, classes are taken outside of that experience, mostly at the *Faculté Notre-Dame (Bernardins)*, the pontifical school that Cardinal Lustiger also founded. Two key elements of Lustiger's vision were the need for a "spiritual year" (conducted at *La Maison Saint-Augustin*)—what is more commonly known now as the propaedeutic year—and the desire to have priestly formation evolve in a pastoral context centered in parish life. While the question of a spiritual or propaedeutic year has become a feature of various seminary programs around the world—and indeed is required according to the new *Ratio* (59–60)—I am not aware that other aspects of the parish-based model have been duplicated in many places. In fact, it was quite evident at its founding that the Congregation for Catholic Education, which was then charged with oversight of seminary formation, was not favorable to this model. I remember a time in the 1980s when the Sulpicians in the United States attempted to design a similar program, at the urging and with the support of a local bishop, but the Holy See did not approve it, and it was never implemented. Be that as it may, the Paris model does exist, though one has to search the writings of Cardinal Lustiger to find many of the details of the program enunciated.[14]

While the exposure to parish life early in seminary formation has certain advantages, some see disadvantages in this model. In particular,

---

13. Some seminarians for the Archdiocese of Paris reside in a formation house in Brussels, Belgium (Notre-Dame de la Strada) and take classes at the Institut d'Etudes Théologiques (IET).

14. For more information, one can consult the website: https://www.seminairedeparis.fr/-Les-etudes-.html#.WlCa2jdG3IU.

there is no formation community as such, since everything is oriented to the local parish, and the formation "team"—if it can be called such—operates primarily by "personnel file," making decisions on the basis of written recommendations from each house director rather than on the team's concrete experience of each seminarian.

D. Part-Time Model

Yet another model, which is unique and unusual, is found, as far as I know, only in France. It is called Séminaire Groupe de Formation Universitaire (GFU, founded in 1967) and constitutes a "part-time" seminary formation program for the philosophy level only (first cycle).[15] Having celebrated its fiftieth anniversary in 2017, it permits young men who are in various programs of professional studies at universities to complete these studies while fostering their priestly vocation and being formed on a part-time basis throughout the year. There are formation gatherings for seven weekends per year, a ten-day summer experience, retreats, and regular contact with a spiritual director. This approach has always been small (fifteen to twenty seminarians at a time) and exceptional but has permitted a number of young men to nourish their priestly vocation while finishing an advance course of studies in a secular field.

II. Evaluative Comments

In ten years as superior general of the Sulpicians, I have had occasion to visit all the Sulpician seminaries around the world, as well as other seminaries and houses of formation. One of my duties obviously is to evaluate the effectiveness of seminary formation in Sulpician contexts and to make recommendations for improvements. These

---

15. See the website at http://www.seminairegfu.fr/ and https://www.facebook.com/seminairegfu/. It is officially described as "une formation en alterance" and is approved for the first cycle by the French Episcopal Conference.

are identified through periodic "canonical visitations" as required by the Holy See and the Sulpician *Constitutions*. There are strengths and weaknesses in every model. The question is to decide whether the weaknesses seriously impact the final "product," if you will, of highly motivated, fully formed, well integrated, holy priests who are good shepherds configured to the Lord Jesus Christ himself (RF 68). So, I offer a few evaluative comments here as a preliminary to the final topic—challenges for the future.

My first comment is that there are numerous variations of these four principal models I have proposed.[16] The main reason seems to be a desire to modify this or that aspect of a given model to improve the quality of priestly formation in an individual context. This is a healthy development. Indeed, I think the promulgation of a new *Ratio*— which is admittedly very consistent with the Sulpician model—is advantageous because it will force episcopal conferences around the world to confront directly the quality of priestly formation in the twenty-first century. All of us in the ministry of priestly formation now have a guiding document to help evaluate in an honest and objective manner the effectiveness of our current programs of priestly formation. We should also note that the *Ratio* itself was the result of a long and extensive worldwide consultation, and so it already has been shaped to a degree by the diversity of situations encountered around the world. Since it is a universal program that must be adapted to local programs of priestly formation, it clearly does not address every single situation that might be encountered.

A second comment concerns numbers of seminarians. Virtually everyone recognizes that numbers of priestly vocations in the

---

16. For example, programs of the Neocatechumenate (with numerous Redemptoris Mater seminaries around the world), Institut d'Etudes Théologiques (IET) in Brussels, Ars, Prado, Mission de France, Communauté de Saint Martin, and others have adapted aspects of seminary formation to suit the needs of their respective groups.

northern hemisphere have declined in recent decades, while those in the southern hemisphere are growing. If on the one hand, one can legitimately question whether a seminary of five, ten, or fifteen seminarians really provides an adequate "community of formation" as the *Ratio* calls for (RF 188), likewise one can pose the question of whether real quality formation in a seminary of more than two hundred and fifty, four hundred, or five hundred seminarians can be truly accomplished with the small number of formators present in those houses. How well known are the seminarians in such a context? How much contact could there be between each seminarian and his formator or team of formators? How could a superior (rector) be prepared to make a judgment of readiness for the next stage of formation or for ordination with such a number? So, at both ends of the spectrum—too few and too many seminarians—one can legitimately pose questions of adequacy of priestly formation.

My third comment addresses the diverse circumstances that exist around the world, which impact the quality of seminary formation. We need to be realistic. In so many of the developing countries I have visited, there is a serious lack of *basic* resources with which to do seminary formation. How can one take advantage of resources, for instance, such as the website of the Congregation for the Clergy,[17] when one cannot even be assured of having electricity throughout the day? In one of our seminaries in Zambia, we have had to purchase expensive generators just to ensure electricity for the refrigerators and freezers to preserve the stored food, let alone to provide some access once in a while to the internet for email when the electricity goes down, which can last for hours at a time on any given day.

Even more serious is the lack of books and journals in many countries. Even well-developed countries like China and Vietnam have a dearth of modern, printed materials that seminarians can access, especially in their own language. I know of seminaries where virtually

---

17. See http://www.clerus.va/content/clerus/en.html.

the only printed resource the seminarians receive for personal use when they enter the seminary is the breviary, and perhaps a Bible. Otherwise, few philosophical and theological books are available to them except in well-worn, limited, and often dated materials found in libraries, which themselves are often poorly equipped. How can one ensure real quality intellectual formation when many basics are simply lacking? Add to this the problem of underdeveloped primary and secondary educational systems in some countries; there is also the challenge of lack of proper academic skills for advanced philosophical and theological studies.

Another lack one finds in many places, except perhaps North America and Europe, is the dearth of resources for human formation. Psychological tools, for instance, highlighted in the *Ratio* (RF 191–196), are often distrusted or simply do not exist in formats adapted to the wide diversity of cultures and languages around the world. In such circumstances, one has to become very creative to apply the universal vision of what constitutes high-quality human formation.

My fourth point is an observation about the general quality of priestly formation around the world. One of the most impressive aspects of my visits to many seminaries and dioceses is the basic goodness I have found. By and large, seminary formation teams are honest, dedicated, hardworking, and faithful formators who are truly trying to do their best to form future priests. Often what is lacking, however, is any kind of in-depth formation training for formators. Sometimes, because of a lack of trained personnel, bishops name young priests as seminary formators without any kind of preparation. Almost every year as superior general, we have received requests to help out in seminaries around the world precisely because of this lack of formation resources, but we ourselves are stretched to meet all these needs.

In addition, despite serious differences of culture and available resources, generally I have found seminarians universally to be good-hearted, malleable, sincere young men who desire to become worthy priests. In some areas where poverty is prevalent, one has to be careful about seminary admissions because of mixed motivations. But overall, I do not see existential differences in seminarians from one country to another. One finds some very brilliant seminarians and some who struggle to master basic academic concepts. There are many devout seminarians whose moral and spiritual life are clearly in order, and then there are some who make one wonder how they were admitted to seminary. Almost all seminarians show interest in pastoral service, but some have real limitations on a human sphere that reinforce concretely the importance of human formation as foundational (RF 94). Most really want to serve God and God's people. I also admire the bishops in these regions who attempt to improve the quality of priestly formation in ways that meet the needs of the local church, despite limited resources of all kinds. Thus, they constantly seek outside assistance to improve their formation programs and are often open to suggestions of ways to move forward. It is this aspect of all-around "goodness" that ultimately gives me hope that priestly formation in the future, whatever changes it may need or may encounter, will provide good workers for the vineyard of the Lord.

III. Challenges for the Future

With these models and some evaluative comments behind us, we turn now to some challenges in priestly formation for the future.

One challenge is to avoid compartmentalization of all the dimensions of priestly formation, especially the four key ones (human, spiritual, intellectual, and pastoral). This, in fact, is a concern of some formators with regard to the propaedeutic year. Although I personally favor such a year in most cases, especially because the present cultural context of a highly secularized world has made such a huge impact on young people, nevertheless one must be careful not to define it solely as a spiritual year. Properly done with a mix of human formation, very basic classes in Catholic faith and Bible, good liturgy, introduction to a wide variety of prayer styles, and good individual and group formation sessions, the propaedeutic year prepares young men to enter seminary with the needed background they would otherwise lack. But if it is viewed only as a spiritual year, almost like a novitiate, the risk can be that they enter seminary with unrealistic expectations of the daily rhythm of life. They sometimes find it hard to accomplish all their responsibilities and still find time for daily prayer. They can be thrown off balance by the intense schedule of the modern seminary. Of course, parish life can also be highly demanding. Without proper attention to personal discipline and good time management, seminarians and priests alike can fall into bad habits that will not sustain them in the long run. The key, I think, is a balanced lifestyle, but not everyone is equally adept at finding his equilibrium.

Another challenge is the need to find better means to transition seminarians from seminary into the priesthood. Most of the current seminary models do a fairly good job of addressing the major components of priestly formation. I am less sanguine about their ability to help third- and fourth-year theology students adapt to their looming priestly identity. More thought can be given to this area, and I would include in this issue the first few years of ordained ministry. Some dioceses have worked out a good mentoring system that aids the process, and some have formal group sessions of young priests to help sustain them. But this is an area where seminaries should have some input and may provide a resource in such a fashion that it is not simply a continuation of the seminary experience, which would make ongoing formation very unattractive to most priests.

The third challenge concerns a host of practical issues that can be best expressed by a series of questions that should be asked in light of the diversity of formation models.

- How does the ideal of a "true formative community" (RF 3, 90, 188) get actualized? With the *Ratio*, I view the communal element as key in seminary formation, but not every model addresses this issue equally well.

- How does a program promote effective integration of all the elements of seminary formation (RF 3, 7, 89, 92, etc.)? This has been, and remains, one of the thorniest aspects of priestly formation—integration. How do we form fully integrated priests? What system provides the perfect blend of human, spiritual, intellectual, and pastoral formation that makes a priest a good shepherd?

- How does one ensure quality human formation as the base of all priestly formation (RF 94, 191–96) in the diversity of cultural contexts found around the world? What role can psychological resources play in human formation, especially in areas where psychological tools are sparse, are considered suspect, or are almost nonexistent?

- Given the diverse roles women play in various cultures, and given the high presence of women in parochial situations worldwide, how can priestly formation ensure proper roles for women in seminary programs, as called for by the *Ratio* (RF 95, 151)?

- Can we identify "best practices" in seminary formation that might serve as good role models for seminaries in various parts of the world?[18] As indicated above, most seminary programs are variations on basic models. Can we nonetheless identify those programs that seem to be most effective to help existing models to adapt and apply them to their own situations?

- How does the seminary combat the tendency toward clericalism and careerism, which is one of the continuing problems in the priesthood and which Pope Francis has regularly condemned (RF 33, 42)?

---

18. See the chapter by Rev. John Kartje of Mundelein Seminary in Chicago, Illinois, for an intriguing model, which is based upon a longstanding and successful program developed at St. Paul Seminary in Minneapolis, Minnesota.

- How does the seminary promote engagement in the world that promotes integration in the pastoral arena while safeguarding a certain distance to permit self-reflective formation in a tranquil environment? Should the seminary be more integrated in parochial life or be kept separate? The *Ratio* clearly sees the pastoral dimension as the place where the other three dimensions of formation take root and produce fruit, but finding the right formula to introduce concrete pastoral experiences to seminarians is elusive. In the US context, the pastoral year has proven to be a very useful tool in seminary formation, but it adds another year of formation and is not obligatory.

- How does seminary formation promote adult, responsible behavior in seminarians and help them to avoid reverting to a more adolescent style of life? One of the problems I have encountered regularly is the tendency of institutional life in seminaries to force a certain reversion in the maturation process. Formation should promote adult, responsible behavior that holds men accountable, rather than emphasizing sheer conformity to a set of external rules.[19]

- How can seminaries promote a better implementation and healthier attitude toward the explicit connection between initial and ongoing formation of priests so clearly enunciated in the revised *Ratio* (RF 80–81)? Creating an understanding of formation as a lifelong need in the priesthood is a big hurdle

---

19. This is one of the findings of studies analyzing why priests engaged in sexual abuse of minors and boundary violations with adults. See, for example, the lengthy and detailed research of Desmond Cahill and Peter Wilkinson, *Child Sexual Abuse in the Catholic Church: An Interpretive Review of the Literature and Public Inquiry Reports* (Melbourne, Australia: RMIT University, 2017). Earlier studies in the United States and Ireland had also, in part, found that a lack of attention to human formation in earlier decades had enabled men with immature, underdeveloped, or aberrant human tendencies to enter priesthood.

to surmount, since seminarians often do not perceive the need and are anxious to finish formation as rapidly as possible, and since many priests themselves find it difficult to fit it into their multiple responsibilities.

These are but some of the practical issues that seminary formators will need to confront as the future unfolds. Some of them are neuralgic and will require deft handling, but they all constitute part of the challenge of ensuring quality priestly formation in the twenty-first century.

Conclusion

To draw this chapter to a close, let me turn to an area of my own formation, namely, biblical studies. For many years, I taught Old Testament wisdom literature, for which I retain a great fondness. One of the underappreciated books in that corpus of biblical literature is surely Qoheleth (Ecclesiastes). Known as *the* skeptic of the Old Testament, the unknown author opines early in his book: "What has been is what will be, / and what has been done is what will be done; / there is nothing new under the sun. / Is there a thing of which it is said, / 'See, this is new'? / It has already been, / in the ages before us" (Eccl 1:9-10).

Granted, Qoheleth's perspective might be a bit cynical for those who think they have the ability to reinvent the wheel, but I wonder if his words are not pertinent to seminary formation. In conversations with bishops and some formators, I have sometimes had the impression they are looking for the new "silver bullet" that will address all the neuralgic issues that face priestly formation. In light of the ongoing aftermath of the sexual abuse scandals, this concern is understandable. But having examined *in situ* many seminaries around the world during a ministry of nearly forty years in priestly formation, I really wonder if there exists some totally new concept that hits the mark.

Just when we think we have reinvented seminary formation, it is then we should recognize that, in reality, we have only created variations on a theme. I do not believe there is any one definitive model of seminary formation, but I do believe some models are better than others, primarily because of the fruit they produce. Does not the gospel say, "You will know them by their fruits" (Matt 7:16)? It is the quality of priests who enter ministry configured to Jesus Christ, the Eternal High Priest, that tells the story. That is what we should be looking at and evaluating.

One of the aspects of the revised *Ratio Fundamentalis Institutionis Sacerdotalis* that appeals to me is its starting point of the "gift of a vocation" and its desired goal of forming "missionary disciples" (RF 3). A priestly vocation begins as a "gift" and a "call" but it ends as an incarnate expression of Christ himself ministering to his needy flock, preaching the good news of healing, of mercy, and of love. Seminary formation needs constantly to adapt to new realities and to refine methods of formation going forward. But we should not be naïve. Apart from the rare, truly original concept that can arise unexpectedly from time to time, I think we formators must rather seek down-to-earth ways to make more efficient that which has, over the centuries since the Council of Trent, rendered a great service to the church. To this end, it is worth reflecting on how to improve seminary models of priestly formation to serve the church in the twenty-first century.

Chapter Nine

Forming the Parish-Priestly Integrated Identity

John Kartje

While "integration" of the four dimensions of priestly formation is universally recognized as one of the central goals of any Catholic seminary system, it is critical to remember that the ultimate objective is not the integration of seminary *programs* but rather the interior integration that occurs *within the man himself*, as his authentic priestly identity takes form (whether diocesan or religious).

This essay reflects the perspective of a diocesan seminary in the United States: the University of Saint Mary of the Lake, whose primary aim is to form men to be diocesan parish priests.[1] In the following, we will explore attempts to create a culture among faculty and students that is singularly focused on the mission of helping each seminarian to interiorly integrate the full range of experiences he acquires throughout his years of seminary formation.

---

1. The university is more commonly known as "Mundelein Seminary," after the third archbishop of the Archdiocese of Chicago, Cardinal George Mundelein, who constructed the seminary in 1921, approximately forty miles northwest of the city of Chicago.

"Feed Them Yourself": An Apostolic Exhortation for Seminary Integration

In a well-known gospel scene, Jesus and the disciples are faced with a large, hungry crowd, with seemingly no means to feed them. Feeling helpless, the disciples appeal to Jesus' authority: "Send them away so that they may go into the surrounding country and villages and buy something for themselves to eat." But Jesus confidently replies: "You give them something to eat" (Mark 6:36-37).

While we understandably tend to focus on the miracle, perhaps the primary lesson to be gleaned here by seminary formators lies in the brief exchange between the master and his disciples which precedes it.

Jesus has good reason to be confident in the disciples: he has taught them, prayed with them, and experienced life with them in a wide variety of circumstances and encounters. He has witnessed their growth, their successes and their failings. In short, he has accompanied them faithfully throughout the journey of his public ministry in Israel. The desired goal of this accompaniment, even if not yet realized, is that the disciples should be able to fully integrate what they have learned from Jesus into the fruit of their prayer with him, so that they might more faithfully love and be present to those whom Jesus loved, and in the way that he loved them.

Such a dynamic of accompaniment is modelled by the Congregation for the Clergy in their description of the principal purpose of seminary formation:

> The fundamental idea [of formation] is that Seminaries should form missionary disciples who are "in love" with the Master, shepherds "with the smell of the sheep," who live in their midst to bring the mercy of God to them. Hence every priest should always feel that he is a disciple on a journey, constantly needing an integrated formation, understood as a continuous configuration to Christ.[2]

---

2. Congregation for the Clergy, *The Gift of the Priestly Vocation: Ratio Fundamentalis Institutionis Sacerdotalis* (London: CTS Publications, 2017) 3.

The key principle is that identity and integration are inextricably intertwined. Whether it is a fisherman becoming an apostle or a seminarian becoming a priest, it is within the man's identity that the process of integration unfolds. As noted above: the *man himself* becomes interiorly more integrated (continuously "configured to Christ"), not the programs to which he is subjected.

Three Levels of Seminary Integration

Insofar as integration is a primary focus of seminary formation, it is important to recognize that integration happens on multiple levels: the integration of the seminary into its diocese (or dioceses, in the case of regional seminaries); the integration of the four dimensions of seminary formation as laid out in *Pastores Dabo Vobis* (hereafter, PDV); and the integration of the seminary faculty (both the integration of each faculty member into the entire body of formators and the interior integration within each faculty member's own mind and heart). When these three levels of integration are functioning well, seminarians are effectively accompanied by their professors and formators throughout their theologate tenure.

Integration of the Seminary into the Diocese

Even though the seminary is preparing men to be priests in the diocese, it is sometimes surprising just how remote the relationship between the diocese and its seminary can be. It would not be unusual for a typical parishioner to be unable to name the seminary at which her parish priest was formed. This is hardly what is desired. Indeed, the Second Vatican Council envisions a beautiful and intimate connection between the local bishop (and his presbyterate) and the seminary community:

> The bishop, by his keen and affectionate care, should encourage the seminary staff and show himself a true father in Christ to the students. Finally, all priests should look on the seminary as the very

heart of the diocese and should gladly help and support it. (*Optatam Totius* 5; emphasis added)

The metaphor "heart of the diocese" is powerful and formative. A heart in isolation, beating by itself, is dangerously misplaced. A heart is only of value if it is well integrated into a host body, taking in blood, replenishing it with new life, and sending it out to be life-giving. To be sure, a seminary takes in men from the diocese, helps them to be infused by Christ's Spirit in the particular transformation of Holy Orders, and then sends them out to bring new life to the very same parishes from which they first were sent. But if this heart is to be truly integrated into its diocesan body, the relationship needs to be nurtured along many pathways.

The diocese ought to be significantly involved in screening potential seminary candidates in a manner that extends beyond the usual efforts of the vocation office. The people whom a newly ordained priest would be shepherding, and shepherding alongside of, should be able to offer their assessment of the man's suitability to become a shepherd in the first place. In the Archdiocese of Chicago (and in many other dioceses), an "Admissions Board" is employed to assist the diocesan Vocation Director in screening potential seminarians.

Comprising laypeople, as well as diocesan parish priests, and drawn from a representative sampling of the diocesan demographics, the board offers a non-binding recommendation on the candidate to the bishop and the vocation office. Board members offer their perspectives on such qualities as the man's emotional and social relational abilities, his capacity for collaboration with laypeople, his views on the local church, and so forth. The board can be helpful in identifying a man who seems hostile toward women or the laity in general, or evinces a sense of entitlement or dismissiveness toward parish priests, or just simply lacks basic social skills. The board's insights have proved valuable in helping to recognize men who might need further preparation before undertaking seminary formation (or, in some cases, who cannot be recommended for pursuing a priestly vocation at all).

In addition to assisting with the seminarian admissions process, the diocese can form abiding relationships with the seminary by means of various diocesan organizations, such as women's councils, the family ministry office, the Catholic schools department, etc. Rather than a perfunctory visit by seminarians to such groups, these organizations should be actively engaged with the seminary formators to provide regular instruction, feedback, and exposure to real-life conditions within the diocese. Although many seminaries provide "field education" or apostolate assignments for their students, these placements and the processing of the students' experiences at the sites are often not as well-integrated as they could be into the overall four-year formation cycle. Ideally, such engagements with diocesan leadership would incrementally deepen as the man progressed through his years of theology study.

Another way that the seminary can better embrace its role as the heart of the diocese is through a deeper awareness of the needs and challenges facing newly ordained priests in their parishes. It is crucial that the seminary understands its role as one stage in a continuum which stretches from a man's first vocational discernment through his years as a retired priest. At Mundelein Seminary, the rector and his staff coordinate closely with both the diocesan office for ongoing formation and the vocation office to regularly assess how well prepared the seminary programs are to receive the current generation of incoming candidates, and also how well they function in preparing newly ordained priests to meet the needs and challenges of the contemporary diocesan parish. The goal of such coordination is to ever more accurately situate the seminary at the heart of the diocese, particularly with an eye toward the evolving needs of the local church and resisting the temptation to settle for an "ossified heart" that rests complacently upon its past operations.

Finally, if the seminary is ever to be fully integrated into the diocese, it is imperative that the laity and the clergy throughout the local parishes see themselves as filling a necessary and critical role in the formation of seminarians. This role should not be understood as simply a helpful supplement to seminary formation; rather, it should be presented, encouraged, and widely understood as a fundamental responsibility that every Catholic helps to shoulder. First and foremost, the parishes need to be praying for the success of the mission of the seminary. It can be shocking, sometimes, to realize how infrequently prayer is mentioned in conjunction with diocesan support of seminary formation. In addition, every priest should be encouraged by his brother priests and his bishop to both foster vocations and to mentor and support current seminarians. Similarly, lay parishioners should be reminded of their unique responsibility to help seminarians develop in their vocations, particularly in the areas of the human and pastoral dimensions. One means for this formation to happen is through the selective placement of seminarians into parish assignments (see the discussion of the "teaching parish program" below).

Furthermore, seminary-diocese integration can benefit greatly from the regular presence, at appropriate times, of parish priests and laypersons on the seminary campus. Such participation can enhance the curriculum of a wide range of academic classes and formation sessions, from Christology (e.g., How is the incarnation manifested in the average parish?), to ecclesiology and canon law (e.g., How does a parish community constitute—both spiritually and canonically—the Body of Christ?), to sacramental theology and praxis (e.g., How is the theology of marriage best witnessed in a baptism preparation meeting?), to name but a few. The witness, challenge, and support from parishioners in the seminary classrooms could bring an integrative component that is currently lacking in many courses.[3]

---

3. Such a presence, if thoughtfully introduced at appropriate times, need not be disruptive to the overall flow of the class, be it an academic course or formation session. At Mundelein Seminary, we are still in the early stages of engaging the laity across the full range of departmental class offerings. The principal challenges

All of these relationships collectively serve to strengthen the symbiotic connection between the diocese and its seminary heart. Within the seminary itself, a multivalent series of integrations need to happen to achieve the proper interior configuration to Christ that is desired for each seminarian individually. We now consider these in turn.

Integration of the Four Dimensions of Priestly Formation

Regarding the four dimensions of priestly formation outlined in *Pastores Dabo Vobis*, the fifth edition of the *Program for Priestly Formation* (the *Ratio Nationalis* governing all priestly formation programs in the United States; hereafter, PPF) could not be more clear in identifying the spiritual dimension as the one which integrates and unifies the others: "Since spiritual formation is the core that unifies the life of a priest, it stands at the heart of seminary life and is the center around which all other aspects are integrated."[4] What this means, in a practical sense, is that a seminary staff ought to be able to identify the spiritual foundation or purpose behind every seminary program or activity. That foundation or purpose will be clearer on certain occasions than others, but it ought never to be absent. Any sense of "competition" among the dimensions (or among the faculty who are primarily responsible for overseeing the various dimensions!) must be rejected in the strongest possible terms.

Consider, for example, how *Pastores Dabo Vobis* insists that intellectual formation must flow out of the learner's relationship with the Lord if it is ever to be useful in a pastoral setting: "To be pastorally effective, intellectual formation is to be integrated with a spirituality marked by a personal experience of God. In this way a purely abstract

---

encountered have entailed working through adjustments to traditional pedagogy, and seeking the optimal amount of in-class presence for the visitors, without creating a distraction or disruption of the desired pace of the classes.

4. United States Conference of Catholic Bishops, *Program for Priestly Formation*, 5th ed. (Washington, DC: USCCB, 2006), 115.

approach to knowledge is overcome in favor of that intelligence of heart which knows how 'to look beyond,' and then is in a position to communicate the mystery of God to the people" (PDV 51).

Classroom Pedagogy. Pragmatically, there is no one exclusive style of pedagogy that invites the seminarian "to look beyond" the confines of his text or classroom, and here is where a Spirit-infused creativity can flourish within the seminary community. One method that several of the Mundelein faculty members employ is simply to pause the lecture or discussion occasionally and invite the students to prayerfully reflect on how they are encountering the Lord in the midst of the lesson at hand. Obviously, this is only a fruitful exercise if the seminarian is (1) growing in his spiritual life via regular engagement with spiritual direction and prayer, and (2) seriously engaging the intellectual material presented in the readings and lectures.

Another approach is to regularly ask the seminarian to draw upon experiences he has had in his parish assignment (which will always entail some form of a "personal experience of God" [cf. PDV 51], whether through encounters with parishioners, or in prayer at the parish) as a means of contextualizing what is being studied in the classroom that day. This is much more than simply fashioning "real-world examples" that illustrate the more abstract theology. Rather, it is honoring the fact that a living encounter with Christ is multifaceted: whether in person or in text, whether in parish ministry or in seminary class discussion.

These examples illustrate but a few of the possibilities for integration among the four dimensions of priestly formation that can occur within the traditional seminary classroom, working with the traditional seminary course material (Christology, Ecclesiology, Soteriology, etc.).

Parish-Based Integration. In most seminaries, classroom pedagogy is supplemented by various types of "field education" experiences. These can range from weekly or bi-weekly pastoral encounters (e.g., visits by the seminarian to a local healthcare facility) to a full yearlong parish immersion internship in the seminarian's home diocese.

For a man who is preparing for diocesan priesthood, special focus ought to be afforded to parish assignments. The *Ratio* makes this clear:

> Much attention should be given to the settings in which the seminarians will carry out their pastoral placements. In particular, *"when it comes to choosing places and services in which candidates can obtain their pastoral experience, the parish should be given particular importance for it is a living cell of local and specialised pastoral work in which they will find themselves faced with the kind of problems they will meet in their future ministry."* (RF 124; original emphasis, as cited in PDV 58)

It is both *in* the parish and *from* the parish that the four dimensions can be most fruitfully integrated within the man. That is, the parish can serve as a sort of formational "laboratory" wherein the seminarian's encounters with parishioners and typical (or extraordinary) parish situations provide opportunities for him to synthesize all that he has been acquiring through his classroom studies (both intellectual and pastoral), his prayer, and his growing human development as a man on the path toward ordination. Similarly, he should be able to transfer the experience of those encounters from the parish back into the seminary, enriching his capacity to develop and deepen the relationship between his study, his prayer, and his social and emotional growth.

Several opportunities for parish engagement are typically offered at theologates in the United States. Some seminaries integrate a full pastoral year (or a full semester) into their curriculum, during which the seminarian is completely immersed into a parish, living with a pastor who mentors him through an internship that is structured by guidelines from the seminary. In addition to internships, most seminarians complete their final year of theology studies as a transitional deacon, assigned to a parish near the seminary. They live at the seminary during the week and continue taking classes and participating in formation sessions, but on weekends they minister in their parishes.

A third possibility for integration of the four dimensions via parish engagement is a "teaching parish program." The basic concept entails each seminarian being assigned to a specific parish for the duration of his seminary tenure (as opposed to a one-year or one-semester internship). At least once per week, the student travels to the parish to engage in a specific ministry and participate in the parish liturgies. The seminary may require that the parish ministry follow a set "curriculum" for each year of study (e.g., first-year theology students might focus on sacraments of initiation, second-year students focus on religious education, and so forth).

While the pastor of each teaching parish assumes primary oversight of the seminarian assigned to him, a critical component of the program is the formation of a lay parishioner committee which is tasked with accompanying the seminarian throughout his time in the parish. This committee, comprising a representative cross section of the parish membership, offers the student valuable feedback on his performance, but it also supplies unique insights into the working of the parish—its strengths and challenges—from a perspective that only the laity can provide. Over time, as trust deepens between the seminarian and his parish committee, the group becomes a formational resource for the student that can powerfully supplement (but never supplant) the regular seminary support staff of spiritual directors and formation advisors. In conversations with them, he gains a sense of his ability to integrate his expanding grasp of theological concepts into the language and presentation style necessary for the diverse range of audiences he will encounter, from schoolchildren to highly accomplished professionals. By leading the parishioners in prayer, and by prayerfully contemplating how the Spirit is moving in his own heart when he interacts with them, the seminarian increasingly becomes "configured to Christ," the goal of integrated formation.

In implementing the teaching parish program at Mundelein Seminary, we initially contemplated leveraging the vast diversity of parish demographics that is found throughout the Archdiocese of Chicago by assigning the seminarians to a different parish for each of their four years in seminary. Such a model could give them exposure to several different socio-economic parish environments. We ultimately opted for a single-parish, long-term experience rather than offering greater variety and shorter exposure times.[5] That decision speaks to the heart of the dynamic of integration among the four dimensions of priestly formation. Insofar as the spiritual dimension is the core around which all the other dimensions are centered, that dimension is best nurtured through the deepening of authentic relationships between the seminarian and the people among whom he is serving.

Such deep relationships require time, patience, and trust to adequately develop. It would be difficult to create a supportive environment for that dynamic to unfold if the man were relocating every nine months, especially if he were experiencing significant shifts in parish culture. It takes time for the shepherd to truly smell like his sheep. It is true that a diocesan priest is often called upon to change assignments abruptly and to embrace a new parish that may differ considerably from his previous one. But during the time of growing configuration to Christ (i.e., during the years of major seminary), it is critical to establish a well-integrated foundation precisely so that the priest can later weather the spiritual storms that are likely to arise due to the rapidly shifting environments in which he is often asked to serve.

At a purely practical level, we might also note that by spending several years in a single parish, a seminarian is likely to witness major stages in the "life cycle" of the parish. For example, over the course of four years the seminarian may well experience a change in pastor, significant parish staff personnel changes (hiring, firing, retirement), budgetary issues (capital campaigns, deficit spending, etc.), or the

---

5. I wish to express deep gratitude to the pastoral faculty of both St. Francis de Sales Seminary (Milwaukee, Wisconsin) and The St. Paul Seminary School of Divinity (St. Paul, Minnesota) who graciously shared with us their collective wisdom and experience gained from operating teaching parish programs for many decades.

loss of key parishioners due to death or relocation. Only if the seminarian is well known and trusted by the community is he likely to be intimately involved with the parish's transition through such times of change. That level of involvement can significantly enhance his priestly formation.

Theological Reflection. It is no exaggeration to say that the success or failure of any attempt at formational integration rests upon the quality of the seminarian's practice of theological reflection. Here, the man is invited and challenged to place into dialogue every aspect of his seminary experience. In effective theological reflection, each student draws upon his natural strengths within the four dimensions of priestly formation so that he might deepen his engagement in areas where he is timid or weak. For example, a man with a natural proclivity for intellectual pursuits cannot remain in abstraction but must find a way to apply the theological concepts with which he feels familiar to actual encounters he has had during his time in the parish (encounters with which he may not feel comfortable at all). Similarly, the seminarian who easily engages others in conversation or ministry, but eschews trying to master theological principles, must make the effort to deepen his grasp of theology so that he might better comprehend the true christological or ecclesiological depths of the seemingly simple encounters he is having.

At Mundelein Seminary (as at most seminaries), students take formal courses in theological reflection where they are taught specific techniques to help them integrate all elements of their formation. Furthermore, several times a semester they gather in small groups to practice theological reflection on brief scenarios they have written (100–150 words), describing encounters from among their experiences in their teaching parishes.

As a seminarian becomes more adept at reflection, he deepens his capacity for grasping and understanding theological concepts in the classroom, as well as his efficacy as a shepherd who can teach the faith and be a bridge to lead others to Christ. Our spiritual directors also notice that as a man becomes more interiorly integrated, his prayer life matures and he engages direction more fruitfully because he is much better at perceiving the movement of the Holy Spirit in his own heart.

We now turn briefly to consider integration as it specifically pertains to seminary faculty.

Integration among Seminary Faculty

It might seem obvious that if a priestly formation program is to succeed at forming men who are interiorly well integrated, then the seminary faculty must itself be well integrated, even as each faculty member focuses on his or her unique role. And yet, faculties often find themselves segmented or siloed for various reasons. The growing degree of specialization throughout contemporary higher education can breed a reluctance to comfortably dialogue with one's colleagues from another department (e.g., systematic theologians not collaborating with Scripture scholars). Many seminary faculty are themselves the product of poorly integrated graduate education systems and thus have never been exposed to the rich possibilities that could be realized. And we should have no illusion concerning real feelings of competition that sometimes exist between "academic faculty" and "formation faculty" over the allocation of time in the *horarium* and funding in the budget for each faculty's programs. Overcoming such segmentation demands regular, and intentional, engagement among faculty and administrators.[6]

The *Ratio* clearly states that oversight of all seminary programs (both formation *and* academic programs) is the responsibility of the rector and the formation faculty:

---

6. We should never underestimate the power of prayer in this context. Seminary faculties should seek out regular opportunities for members to pray with and for each other. It is absolutely imperative that every faculty member (lay and religious) has a spiritual director whom he or she sees regularly.

The intellectual formation of the candidates is the responsibility of the Rector and of the community of formators.[7] With the participation of the "coordinator of intellectual formation" [i.e., "academic dean"], the formators shall ensure the cooperation of the professors and other experts, and shall meet regularly with them, in order to address teaching related matters, so as to *promote more effectively the integral formation of the seminarians.* (RF 141; emphasis added)

The seminary-wide primacy granted to the formation faculty in the *Ratio* would perhaps come as a surprise to many faculty members. And yet, if the goal of seminary formation is a man who is well integrated spiritually, intellectually, humanly, and pastorally, then we should expect that the formators—with their mission of accompanying the seminarian along every step toward ordination—would be the ones with the most direct oversight and assessment of every aspect of seminary life.

Each seminary faculty must seek integration in its own way. We list here several processes followed at Mundelein that are designed to help achieve this goal.

1. A "Faculty Integration Team" (FIT), comprising three formation faculty and three academic faculty members, is appointed by the rector each year. The mission of the FIT is to maintain open and intentional communication with the entire faculty, so as to focus on new ideas or challenges that arise concerning opportunities for the faculty to integrate their efforts toward a unified priestly formation program. The FIT communicates regularly with the rector to help him develop an integration strategy that is responsive to the ever-changing needs of the seminary community. One example of a FIT-led initiative was the organization of an all-seminary formation day exploring the theology, pastoral implications, and spiritual insights

---

7. In the language of the *Ratio*, the "community of formators" corresponds to what is typically referred to as the "formation faculty," as opposed to the "academic faculty."

of *Amoris Laetitia*. This event drew on contributions from both academic and formation faculty, as well as seminary spiritual directors.

2. "Real time communication" is encouraged among the faculty so that potentially problematic issues can be addressed as soon as they surface. Every academic faculty member receives a list of each student's formation advisor, and every formation faculty member has access to the syllabus for every seminary course. This allows professors and formation advisors (and, via the formation advisors, spiritual directors) to consult with one another quickly, should a concern arise, and it prevents a one-sided perspective on a student from developing (e.g., noticing only poor academic performance but being unaware of personal emotional struggles, etc.).

In addition, the entire formation team gathers weekly with the vice rector and rector (when possible) for brief assessments of the state of the community, noting if there are particular formation or academic concerns arising, or if any particular students are in need of assistance. The academic faculty hold similar meetings with the academic dean (and the rector, when possible). Several times per semester, select members of the formation faculty attend the weekly academic meeting (and vice versa). Such regular gatherings further enhance the level of integration across the artificial dividing lines which can grow between the formation and academic spheres.

3. Finally, faculty members themselves are often in need of nurturing their own interior integration, regardless of which department they belong to. It cannot be assumed that in their advanced studies, seminary faculty received instruction that specifically prepared them to serve in support of priestly formation. Most STD programs vary little from their secular PhD counterparts, and there exist few graduate programs that provide training for formation faculty.[8] In

---

8. The Society of St. Sulpice ("Sulpician Fathers") has a long tradition of providing training for seminary faculty; in the United States, some support is provided by offerings from the National Conference of Diocesan Vocation

addition to availing themselves of such offerings as do exist (which the seminary administration strongly supports), faculty participate in several annual in-service days focused on helping them to better contextualize how their own area of expertise can benefit from greater integration with the efforts of their colleagues.

"What I Have I Give You":
An Apostolic Integration Success Story

We began this essay by recounting the disciples' struggle to receive Jesus' confidence in their abilities to meet the needs of a hungry crowd. It would require a long journey of accompaniment through the Paschal Mystery before all the complex pieces of their lives with Jesus and his challenging statements to them "made sense." When Peter encounters the lame man at the Temple after Pentecost, his words bespeak the fruit of his own interior integration. He clearly knows what he lacks (money) and how that frees him to embrace what he possesses: "I have no silver or gold, but what I have I give you; in the name of Jesus . . . stand up and walk" (Acts 3:6).

The sublime blending of humility and confidence evinced in this scene provides as good a witness as any to what a well-integrated program of priestly formation should aspire toward.

Directors and the National Association of Catholic Theological Schools; recently, several of the largest diocesan seminaries in the United States have collaborated to found the Seminary Formation Council, which offers a two-year certificate program specifically oriented toward the training of diocesan seminary formation faculty members.

Chapter Ten

Formation of Priests: Assessing the Past, Reflecting on the Present, Imagining the Future

Hans Zollner, SJ

Know what you are doing, and imitate the mystery you celebrate: model your life on the mystery of the Lord's cross.[1]

At a recent workshop for seminarians, we spoke about their expectations for their future ministry as priests. Along with much enthusiasm for spreading the Gospel and administering the sacraments, many of them voiced their worries about the substantive amount of time and energy that would need to go into administrative matters. One seminarian put into words the desire of many in the room: "We want to be pastors of souls." This longing to accompany the spiritual journey of others is a magnanimous one, and it has remained etched in my mind because it touches the heart of my academic work, which is focused on the formation of those who are occupied with

---

1. From the Rite of Ordination at the presentation of paten and chalice to the newly ordained.

the human and spiritual formation of future pastors. Formators who receive such a candidate face a myriad of questions: How can one assist the maturation of this person so that he achieves his goal of helping others? How may the positive motivations be deepened and selfish motivations purified so that the candidate is truly capable of helpful relationships? How does one educate another to discern and resist potentially harmful or destructive behavior, especially behavior that crosses physical, sexual, psychological, and spiritual boundaries?

Where We Are Coming From: Perceiving the Situation

There is a growing sense of the need to reassess the concept of seminary formation established by the Council of Trent and widely applied for nearly 500 years. Though generally successful in the past,[2] is it adequate and effective today, or are some aspects of it now counterproductive to the primary goals of formation? Until a few decades ago, in Western countries, and still now in many countries of the developing world, the men who entered seminary (on average, eighteen to twenty years old) came from a rather coherent and similar background—a Catholic family, normally with a few siblings, solid catechetical training, and a familiarity with liturgy and traditional devotions. The formation system assumed a solid personality structure, presupposing spiritual, communal, and church-learning qualities that naturally fit into a church environment. The main focus was on strengthening spiritual values and practices as well as imparting sound theological and philosophical intellectual formation.

Formation based on such conditions basically meant providing spiritual input and guidance, taking for granted that seminarians would strive in a self-induced way to actively engage in integrating and living out higher ideals, and that society at large, or at least

---

2. See Stephen J. Rossetti, *Why Priests Are Happy: A Study of the Psychological and Spiritual Health of Priests* (Notre Dame, IN: Ave Maria Press, 2011).

the faith community (including one's own family), would support (and somehow lend legitimacy to) the priestly lifestyle and ministry. In many religious environments—at least until the Second Vatican Council—this was accompanied by devotional and ascetic practices that were meant to model, strengthen, and exercise ways of living out one's religious commitment. It seems that as long as there was a social and ecclesial environment to sustain such a lifestyle and vocational orientation, men—even those who showed signs of weaknesses or shortcomings—received sufficient input to continue their commitment within the range of normal limitations.

That system, which worked well with many candidates who were strong, or at least sufficiently solid, nevertheless obviously failed on too many occasions. This was especially evident when (1) there was a severely emotionally, relationally, or sexually impaired personality that managed to pass through all formation stages without being dismissed; (2) compliance to norms and superiors was considered one of the most important criteria for promotion (and not sincerity in efforts to grow humanly, spiritually, and academically); and (3) not only the formation setting itself but the entire church environment or context was purposely closed off to the world outside. Such environments often were not subjected to normal, healthy, effective evaluation, supervision, and review. If governed by leaders who felt invested with divine power by virtue of ordination and who acted in an autocratic manner (e.g., by oppressing consciences and asking for blind obedience, while at the same time abusing power, money, and sex) such conduct easily led to cover-up, cultural silence, negligence, and dysfunctional networks, amounting to a counter-testimony to Christian values of devastating proportions.

Of course, the majority of bishops, provincials, and priests in the past lived up to the church's expectation and their own ideals. Yet, it is disturbing to note that despite the formation they received in minor and major seminaries, a significant number of clergy left the priesthood and far too many committed all kinds of abusive behavior, including sexual violence against minors. One must honestly admit that this model of formation frequently did not achieve the results it was striving for.

Where We Are: Dilemmas in Formation

In some countries and seminaries, the situation has changed, and there is now much more attention given to the screening process before admitting new men to the seminary or novitiate. There is greater accompaniment, explicitly taking into consideration affective maturity and sexuality in a broad sense. Yet, in many parts of the world, to my knowledge and firsthand experience, this is still not the case. Not a few bishops, abbots, and provincials speak and act as if they thought that psychology *as such* destroys vocations.[3] However, some of these very same bishops then rely on psychology as the sole argument for decision making (e.g., dismissal) after major difficulties surface in a priest's or seminarian's life.

One reason for this inconsistency is that some formators and bishops are wary of accepting and integrating psychology into the human formation process. They believe that if one pays too much attention to human things, seminarians and novices will discover that they have issues: "The more they talk about sexuality, the more problems they will have." It is a vicious circle: in all likelihood some formators who have personal difficulties in the area of sexuality, affectivity, and relationships are frightened by these aspects of human life; many others do not feel sufficiently equipped to accompany young people in their vocational discernment. Thus, instead of working actively and thoroughly through

---

3. While it is true that some psychological approaches are not compatible with gospel values (e.g., putting self-esteem or self-development at the center of attention), this is not (and, in a really value-neutral perspective, should not be) true for all schools of psychology. See Alessandro Manenti, Stefano Guarinelli, and Hans Zollner, eds., *Formation and the Person: Essays on Theory and Practice*, SIS Supplement 12 (Leuven: Peeters, 2007).

motivational dynamics and affective desires, young men are induced to forcefully repress an integral side of human life or to avoid questions when they arise, which in turn may result sooner or later in all kinds of misbehavior, as well as abandonment of the priesthood. Many seminarians—mostly when they do not feel invited to speak about their issues or when they even fear that talking about doubts or crises will lead to their dismissal—become *submarines*, so to speak: they go under water upon entrance into the formation house, they dive down for the entire duration of formation, trying to make no noise and remain unseen, and they only emerge above water at the right moment (i.e., when the bishop lays his hands on their heads for ordination).

In this way, many years of formation are wasted and unique opportunities for growth are lost. Where young people are challenged as well as helped properly, the fruits can be seen in greater effectiveness of ministry and perseverance in the vocation that God has put in their hearts. What kind of psychology is therefore appropriate in a formation setting? The humanistic approach (encountering others with "unconditional positive regard") is good as a starting point. It is necessary especially for those whose self-esteem and personality structures are not sufficiently developed. But this is not enough for living out the full gospel, because there is an inbuilt tendency in human beings to remain at the level of "I need to enhance myself, and as long as I am happy with me, all is well."

Jesus' call is surely to love oneself, but he calls us also to love others and to love God. What he reveals, even at the cost of his own life, is that the love of others and even of enemies goes beyond self-love. Real fulfillment of self as disciples of Jesus Christ is only possible— paradoxically—in putting the other and God first, reaching out, in loving, in dying to self. The law of the gospel—"whoever loses his life for my sake will gain it"—means there is a cost to following Jesus Christ and imitating his life and his passion in the hope of being granted resurrection with him.

The paradox here is that people need to build up enough self-esteem and personality structure so that they can lose themselves, give themselves, and discover that so long as they are worried about gaining their own gratification, craving self-fulfillment through position or power or money or sex, they will never be satisfied or full. For we can taste, savor, and relish Christian fulfillment only when we experience giving ourselves away. It is far stronger and far more meaningful than what we can procure for ourselves.[4]

How can one grow into such a self that is strong enough to give oneself away in the service of the kingdom of God? An important tool for this is sound asceticism, i.e., the exercise of self-discipline in such a way that one continually learns that one is not in the center of the whole universe, that giving is better than taking, that meaningful renunciation is part of a better human and Christian life. Then the person can come together, becoming more wholesome and healthy, despite—or better, *with*—all the limits and the breaking points that are still there. Compared to their peers' struggles in jobs and relationships, it seems that many seminarians learn rather to be served and to live in a comfortable, exclusive world that has very little to do with the reality of normal people. To many people, this looks more like raising little princes, instead of preparing pastors for the joys and the hardships of sharing their lives with their flocks.

Unfortunately, in my experience, many seminaries do not prepare seminarians well enough for what they will encounter in priestly life, and this is true for all four areas of formation outlined in *Pastores Dabo Vobis* (PDV)[5]—human, spiritual, intellectual, and pastoral.

Human Formation

Human formation, according to Pope St. John Paul II (PDV 43) is the foundation or cornerstone of *all* formation and helps men live

---

4. See Brenda M. Dolphin, *The Values of the Gospel: Personal Maturity and Thematic Perception* (Rome: PUG, 1991).

5. John Paul II, Post-Synodal Apostolic Exhortation *Pastores Dabo Vobis*, 25 March 1992.

out their priestly and religious vocations. Now the abandonment of priestly and religious vocations frequently originates in crises around human affectivity and sexuality, so it is astonishing that this area is not sufficiently addressed in formation before and after the seminary years. It is as if we do not like to seriously analyze this and make decisions accordingly.

Despite the insistence in the *Ratio Fundamentalis Institutionis Sacerdotalis* (*The Gift of the Priestly Vocation*)[6] on involving women in the seminary formation process, there are seminary formators who find this dangerous and possibly detrimental for vocations. This is indicative of an unrealistic and very often harmful attitude, especially since most church attendance is by women and children—so young priests, who have lived in all-male contexts for years, meet with this so-called "danger" and are often unprepared and naive in their attitudes and behavior.

A formator needs to see where challenge (in areas where the seminarians need more growth) and support are to be applied. One can wonder to what extent the Tridentine concept of formation, because of its minimal flexibility in personalizing formation and its closed atmosphere, currently does justice to the reasonable expectations and necessary qualifications that seminarians would have and need today.

Spiritual Formation

Seminarians very often only learn to pray in a formal way and with others, mostly in the Liturgy of the Hours, and they are introduced to the celebration of the Eucharist and other liturgical prayer forms. What many do not receive is an intense introduction to and accompaniment in personal prayer, in prayer that is like talking with a friend (as Teresa of Avila put it).

---

6. Congregation for the Clergy, *The Gift of the Priestly Vocation: Ratio Fundamentalis Institutionis Sacerdotalis* (London: CTS Publications, 2017).

Praying the Liturgy of the Hours together in seminary is far from the reality after initial formation: in most parishes, a priest lives alone, and no one prays lauds and vespers with him. Moreover, many priests who pray the breviary with little existential involvement have not been helped to relate the psalms to their spiritual development and to pray about what is really happening to them. Consequently, prayers become devoid of personal meaningfulness, and then some priests experience a split in their lives; their spiritual lives are disconnected from the ministry in which they are engaged and thriving. Fundamentally, it would be necessary for seminarians to learn how to bring their real lives into their prayer—their thoughts, feelings, ideals, experiences—to prevent the stagnation of spirituality after seminary while the rest of the priests' lives (in which they develop, learn, take responsibility) matures. How much do we help seminarians really live out and develop over a lifetime their friendship with Jesus Christ?

Due to necessary restrictions, I will not address *intellectual formation* and *pastoral formation* at length. Still, one might ask to what extent academic theology is in touch with the urgent questions of today's world, with the queries of normal believers and their need for reasonable ways to respond to an increasingly complex world with rapid changes in communications, science, and business. How does academic and ministerial training of future priests take into account sound relationships and boundaries as well as communication theory and practice (most of what priests do in their ministry is linked to these), introduction to working with groups, methods of peer evaluation, and to lifelong, learner-centered learning? The idea of ongoing formation seems foreign to many new priests. They seem to think that with ordination they are "complete" in their priesthood and no longer need to grow in any other area.

Today we find three basic models of formation in use: the perfection model, the self-realization model, and the integration model. It is quite likely that sometimes they coexist in one seminary because different formators follow different ideas. In the *perfection* model,[7] the priest is somehow just perpetuating the structure, like an element in a machine, while in the *self-realization* model,[8] the priest is basically fulfilling his own perceptions and ideas about church and priesthood without taking into consideration that he necessarily must grow beyond that. In contrast, in the *integration* model, there is a responsible exercise of freedom. This model is realistic and responsible in the sense of learning to live with inner and interpersonal tensions, and growing in a deeper sense of owning oneself and giving oneself at the same time. This model goes to the core of the personality (the heart level), making it more demanding than the other two because it does not avoid tensions through authority or laissez-faire but tries to identify and work through them on the individual, spiritual, and communal levels. As a model of discernment, it presupposes that people are in contact with their inner movements (*mociones*, as St. Ignatius would say) and that they go through a *schola affectus* (a "school of the heart" in which inner movements are neither repressed nor simply released but explored to see where they lead).[9]

---

7. The perfection model is highly idealistic, emphasizing impeccability and striving for what is seen as morally pure and unquestionable. Its insistence on blind obedience and fulfillment of orders prevents men from internally owning their decisions and from critically and rationally entering into a dialogue. Control is valued over freedom, norms over self-responsibility.

8. The key idea in the self-realization model is that every seminarian will discover on his own how to grow and develop, where to go, and what to do. Out of fear of intervening too much or of seeming to be controlling, formators with the laissez-faire idea either believe in self-fulfillment psychology or just want to avoid conflict. In such an environment, needs and desires are not repressed as in the perfection model; nor are they educated and integrated.

9. Hans Zollner, "Core, Criteria and Consequences of the Ignatian Discernment of Spirits," *IGNIS—Ignatian Spirituality in South Asia* 35 (2006): 52–65.

The Journey Ahead: Elements of Education and Formation for Discerning Disciples

It seems that one of the most important questions for our consideration is: What is priesthood all about in today's and tomorrow's world?

Under the conditions of today's society, living priesthood today is, humanly speaking, more challenging than it was a few decades ago. The reality, the profile, and the view of the priesthood have changed. In some aspects it seems to be much more demanding than what used to be the expectation in terms of spiritual depth, professional competence, and relational capacities. On the one hand, there are enormous expectations; on the other hand, any sound person will not expect a priest to be a super-human being. In that sense, as always in history, the most important criterion for how priests are seen by the faithful is whether they are striving to fulfill their ideals to the best of their capacities, and if they fail, whether they are humble enough to admit that and move on (down-to-earthness).

The church needs to discern and decide: What is a priest expected to be and to do? At the moment, a priest does everything in a parish or at least he is responsible for everything—liturgy, spiritual guidance, sacraments, administration, finances, and planning. During seminary formation and, quite frequently, after the seminary, the latter three points are normally not addressed. That means that priests as leaders of parish communities often need to take responsibility for something they are not trained in, to the detriment of the central mission of priesthood. One can detect a fixation on numbers of priests and ordinations, on quantity instead of quality, as if priests would need to fill the gaps that arise; and because of that, the pressing questions are not really considered.

What does all this mean for roles and responsibilities of priests and the sharing of responsibility with the lay faithful? What does it mean for diocesan institutions and ecclesial structures, including parishes, schools, and other sectors like charitable works or healthcare? These are questions that need to be addressed in a wider context of a theology of priesthood and church and that will have repercussions on church law and practical provisions. Within the focus of this chapter, one of the questions that arises is: What is the corresponding vision for the formation of a seminarian and a priest?

Consider the men who are entering seminary today. The average age of seminarians in many Central and Western European seminaries (but also increasingly so in other areas of the world) is about thirty years old or greater. That means they have lived about ten to fifteen years on their own. Many have not only completed their studies, including graduate degrees, but also have years of work experience. Usually they have had academic and/or professional training, either within the ecclesiastical disciplines or in a completely different area, sometimes carrying significant responsibilities within organizations. They have lived in different parts of their home countries, and some have lived abroad. They have a huge amount of life experience, but many of them have had years of very little religious practice. In terms of their relational and sexual lives, it can be assumed that many of them have had intimate relationships and were in stable dating relationships for a number of years. It is also quite likely that they have viewed internet pornography. Normally they have developed longstanding friendships, which they want to continue during and after seminary formation. By the time they finish formation, quite a few of them will be approaching midlife.

Because of these aspects of today's seminary population, very different to the quite homogeneous community of the past, it is essential to diversify formation according to the varied circumstances and backgrounds of candidates to the priesthood. One ought to consider:

- integral human and spiritual life according to the expected levels in the personal, emotional, relational, and sexual areas; the loneliness of diocesan priests and the formation issues surrounding that;

- intellectual capacity to interact with reality in society with the political, economic, and scientific developments that are taking place;

- spiritually free, personalized, and interiorized ways of prayer, learning from tradition, searching for a way to live spirituality in a socially meaningful and ministerially effective way.[10]

Ongoing Formation

It is necessary to invest not only in initial but also ongoing formation. There is more emphasis on initial formation than on ongoing formation. The concept of ongoing formation is foreign to some priests. Maybe they imagine that once theology is finished, formation is complete and they have everything they need. Dioceses and religious congregations rarely instill the idea that after ordination there is still growth that needs to happen. Priests are among the most resistant of professional groups in accepting the idea of the need for ongoing formation. An element in this may be that they mistake the fullness of priesthood received in ordination with the completion of their human, spiritual, and ministerial maturity.

There is the problem of resistance to hearing the same thing over and over, especially to that which regards the area of protection of minors. Many priests do not want to hear about something for which they have already been bashed, or feel indirectly accused, even though they have no direct responsibility and have not committed transgressions.[11]

---

10. Giovanni Cucci and Hans Zollner, *The Church and the Abuse of Minors* (Gujarat: Gujarat Sahitya Prakash, 2013).

11. These priests (who are in the majority) are sometimes referred to as "non-offending priests," as if they are defined by whether or not they have abused minors. See Barry O'Sullivan, *The Burden of Betrayal: Non-Offending Priests and the Clergy Child Sexual Abuse Scandals* (Leominster: Gracewing, 2018).

On top of that, priests feel exposed to general suspicion. If child sexual abuse and its prevention, including reference to professional and pastoral boundaries, are addressed during formation years, the chances are much higher that church authorities will not need to address them after the initial formation stages, which, as everyone involved in dealing with those cases can easily attest, costs an enormous amount of time, nerves, and money—not to mention the criminal behavior, the harm done to young people, and the credibility of the church.

All kinds of formation—initial and ongoing—need clarity, creativity, and perseverance. This is not finished when one has received and developed and promulgated new guidelines for formation. This process—that is, the drafting and revision of national guidelines for priestly formation at the level of bishops' conferences (and to some extent in religious orders and congregations), fleshing out what the *Ratio Fundamentalis Institutionis Sacerdotalis* indicates—will not be complete until suitable structures are put in place and formators are prepared accordingly.

Those documents are often lofty and do not sufficiently take into account the available resources or the challenges that rectors, spiritual directors, and other formators encounter and are willing to talk about when asked in private (e.g., the level of openness of seminarians to talk about their real issues with regard to their need for affection, questions about closeness and distance with others inside and outside the seminary, emotional ups and downs, desires for sexual interaction, and, not infrequently, sexual acting-out before and during seminary formation). Bishops and provincials invest much in intellectual formation and a little in spiritual formation but tend to underestimate and under-resource the human and pastoral formation aspects, which is all the more surprising as vocational crises after ordination in almost all instances are not linked to academic and theological questions, but almost exclusively to human, relational, emotional, and sexual struggles. This ought to be taken into account in national guidelines, honestly admitting that there are real challenges, instead of avoiding them out of fear.

In seminaries, there are very good and willing people, despite the limitations, but the formation system does not seem to offer appropriate support to bring out the best in the capacities of these people. Very often human, spiritual, and pastoral potential is wasted because we do not invest enough in the precious years of preparation for ordination and the years afterward. Church documents presuppose that there is enough personnel and structural or organizational support for the process, but there is almost no place in the world where there are enough formators in the seminary, and those few formators are very frequently not adequately formed for the challenges they face. Whatever we invest (planning, time, and money) in training personnel, in structural formation, and in working on major challenges will pay off mid- and long-term.

Much more needs to be said with regard to a theology of priesthood that takes into account present-day circumstances and endeavors to delineate "Priester *sein*" ("being a priest," distinguished from "acting as a priest"[12]) according to the rite of ordination to the priesthood, which urges the newly ordained: "Know what you do, imitate what you celebrate, and conform your life to the mystery of the Lord's cross." Rethinking the priesthood is all the more urgent as, despite all the questions and shortcomings that we have mentioned, so many people ask for help, guidance, and support on their spiritual and faith journey from those who they believe are themselves searchers of God and his will in this world.

Conclusion

Summarizing the above in a few points, it is presupposed that in all our efforts it is the Lord himself who is the source and the end. The axiom that *God's grace perfects human nature*, Catholic teaching

---

12. See Gisbert Greshake, *Priester sein in dieser Zeit* (Würzburg: Echter, 2005).

since Thomas Aquinas, invites us to do whatever is within our reach, expecting that he will perfect us and our efforts.

Quality over quantity, that would be the *first* point: a joyful priest can "do" an incredible amount; a single sick and implausible priest becomes a nuisance to many. Positions filled by people with significant personal problems will soon be left unoccupied, and much damage will have been done.

Second, good accompaniment of the vocational decision, as well as the entire training period, is of paramount importance for the success of a religious vocation.

Third, today a sustainable vocational decision needs more time and a personalized training path. The people who aspire to a spiritual vocation today have many talents and competencies; others are often underdeveloped, especially those needed for community life. Here, a "modularized" training course could help to "fix" where most of the backlog exists (for example, community skills).

Fourth, dioceses and orders need instructors sufficiently prepared for their task. Just as many years and a lot of money are invested in the training of professors at the seminaries or faculties, so must one invest in the education of rectors, spiritual fathers, and other formators, those who accompany the human and spiritual processes in an important phase of the life of young people, so that the latter can better live up to the great option and vocation that is being a priest of Jesus Christ.

www.ingramcontent.com/pod-product-compliance
Lightning Source LLC
Chambersburg PA
CBHW051943290426
44110CB00015B/2093